HEALING TO

PROSPERITY

Restoration through God's Way and Purpose

Healing is something you do on purpose, something you intend, something you purpose, and something you become--you become healed and therefore you begin your story as a healer to the masses."

ALEX YOUNG, PH.D.

HEALING TO PROSPERITY

Copyright © 2019 by Alex Young, Ph.D.

HEALING TO PROSPERITY

Table of Contents

ACKNOWLEGMENTS

Thankful to God's inspiration which gave me the courage and begin and finish this work. I am thankful to family and friends who were supportive and encouraging through this process while I was working in silence and isolation. I am thankful to my life coach, *Nikisha Ware*, who confronted and challenged me to dig deep and overcome my fears. To the person who took time to edit this work in its rawest form and provide direction without compensation, thanks *Jennifer Spann*. Thankful to my editor, *Ashley Emma*, of Fearless Publishing, who was always accessible whenever I had a question.

FOREWORD

By LaShondra McMillian

Dr. Alex Young, to so many, she listens, advises, and even empathizes with the stories she hear daily. Some stories are so dark and yet similar to her own story.

The story I have come to know in the past few years although I have known Alex since freshman year in college. The quiet valley girl that came from a nice middle class family that displayed a well put together pure and innocent persona. Yes, this is the Alex I knew.

Dr. Young shares her personal life of abuse and wrong relationships and the effects it has had on her. However, she does not stop there, she shares the process of overcoming in the midst of constant reminders. Yet, she presses past the familiar.

I have known Dr. Alex Young for many years as a therapist, friend, and sister in the Lord. I met Alex freshman year at Tougaloo College in the library. It was there in the library that we would spend most of our time discussing relationships and life. In this place is where I got a glance of a caring and compassionate soul who longed to love and be loved.

The quiet valley girl who came from a nice middle class family who displayed a well put together pure and innocent persona was the image that I remembered most. She was always fashionable, graceful, and always exhibited poise. I teased her often as the "valley girl," but little did I know that she had experienced a valley, and it was far from the TV version of a valley girl.

Yet, she never appeared moved by her circumstances. She continued to be a listening ear that empathized and advised others.

As time passed, Alex became more and more authentic about the pain and trauma she experienced. It would be during this time that I really begin to know the strength of my friend and her determination to be victorious through her faith. Her deep desire to know truth and live it is powerful. She exemplifies the life of Christ in many ways as you will see in her reactions to the trauma, hurt, and pain revealed in the book.

As a survivor of sexual and emotional abuse and a servant to homeless, abused, and broken women, I have found the insight from Dr. Young's book to be a great source of healing for myself and others.

Dr. Young, being both a psychologist and woman of faith, shows in this book the need for soul healing through the Spirit. She reveals that the mind and emotions can only be healed through the finished work of the cross that is through the blood of Jesus.

Dr. Young shares her personal life of abuse and wrong relationships and the effects it has had on her. However, she doesn't stop there. She shares the process of overcoming. I recommend this book to anyone who is ready to be real, find healing, and move forward. Let's move forward into destiny and the abundant life of God. It's time to overcome and walk in victory!

INTRODUCTION

"The LORD is my strength and my shield; My heart trusted in Him, and I am helped; Therefore my heart greatly rejoices, And my song I will praise Him." **Psalms 28:7 (NKJV)**

Healing occurs in a place where I did not always recognize. It existed in my spirit, a place of peace and purity that exists within me. My mind pondered over my pain with many questions. I would often think, "How will I ever get over it?" "How is it possible that this happened to me?" or "How could have I have let this happen?" Or the most common question, "Is there something wrong with me which caused this?"

These are the questions that came to mind when I began the process of healing. In my process, I sought professional counsel/therapy, but also sought fervently the voice of God. I sought to hear and listen to His voice. As I cried out at night, I knew God heard me, as the answers were always waiting and appearing in unexpected ways. I saw this was God's way, when reading Psalms 34:17 (HCSB), "The righteous cry out, and the Lord hears, and delivers them from all their troubles." I knew that the Lord heard me, because my spirit felt a peace that led to me to begin this work without fear and doubt. This is something that was already done. Healing was for my receiving, for it had already been given by Jesus Christ, the Lord and Savior.

I am reminded of this in I Peter 2:24 (NKJV): "Who Himself bore our sins in His own body on the tree, that we, having died to sins, might live for righteousness, by whose stripes you were healed." In other words, it tells us that Christ died on the cross for our sins, and by his wounds, we are healed. The power is within us, we just have to acknowledge it and received the power. I was always searching for a way to heal on the outside of myself. I did not understand that healing was always within my reach, I just needed to trust in God. This proximity of healing became more apparent as I drew closer to God. And this is where my journey begins.

As I began writing this book, I did not realize how difficult the process of healing could be. I thought that healing was linear process, but I quickly learned that healing did not occur linearly. It seems that events that promote healing occur in sequences. Healing comes about, like layers on an onion.

At the beginning, I did not know how much emotional pain I was in, or how much pain I was unknowingly holding back. Healing could not and would not begin until I acknowledged the depth of my pain, despite its origin. I did not know the depth my pain or the depth of my denial. I had established a well-formed habit of covering and hiding my pain for the sake of others, telling others, "I am okay" when I really was not.

Therefore, I persisted in hiding my pain, unknowingly, because it had become second nature. I thought I was fine, saying, "Why, of course I am fine, I'm writing a book about healing."

I thought that since I completed my psychotherapy, and things were going well for me in life, I was healed and that I had arrived! Well, sort of.

It was naïve of me to think this was going to be easy. The easy part was saying that there was a problem; the difficult part was acknowledging my true emotions and feelings about the unfortunate series of events which occurred in my life. So I asked myself these questions. If there is no acknowledgment of the problem, how do I know where to start? How do I even know how to heal or what to heal? Even so, I would try to avoid things that reminded me of the traumatic events that caused me pain.

I would retreat and become overwhelmed by "everything" else in my life. There was one particular event in my past that was affecting me in ways I could not have predicted. The way that this trauma affected me was causing me to become overly anxious when with faced with someone who "seemed" overbearing, controlling, and needy too soon, or asking for too much too soon in any type of relationship (i.e., friendship, romantic). I developed a distrust of people. I had the general feeling that a person only wanted something from me when they were showing kindness, thinking, "There has to be a motive." This had been my experience.

Though this may not always be the case, trauma distorts reality at times, and makes you hypersensitive to things which were once neutral. So I retreated, not opening my heart up to anyone for some time until I was able to decipher the nuances of my trauma and that of reality. With this, my healing began with numerous therapy sessions, and an intense, intimate relationship with God. It was then when I began to understand or get a glimpse of the deep love (God's love).

The one traumatic event was not isolated, but it was an accumulation of events which occurred over my lifetime; and I needed "A Healing" in those deep, dark places of my soul. In my case, there were lifetime events which led to the choices which led to encountered trauma in my adulthood. It was a pattern of habit. Some may call it a "generational curse." The term generational curse refers to dysfunctional patterns of behaviors which cause history to repeat itself in families.

My path to healing is one of the reasons why I am writing this book along with other reasons like obedience. So with that being said, this book's purpose is to share with you my journey of healing, hoping that some of these experiences and stories could provide some insight and hope toward purposeful healing in your life.

What I have also come to understand on my journey is that healing is a matter of life and death. You either heal or you die. If it is an emotional death, your body will soon catch up with it. If it is a physical wound, then perhaps your spirit can foster back some life into it. Healing comes from the power within (Spirit). This is the power that we have become unaware of and but do not always acknowledge. My mind (soul) would constantly ponder on why I was not yet be healed, and why I was not better. However, healing comes from the Spirit.

Healing is a step toward life, and pathway to dreams, and dreams are an opening to your destiny. Again I say it: healing is a matter of life and death. Do you want to live or do you want die? What will it be? This is the question you should answer and this is the path which you will choose: a living death or thriving life. I think Andrew Wommack said it best when he teaches on healing: "God wants us all healed."

Wommack explained about how we as individuals are quick to attribute our sickness to God or from God as a lesson or a punishment, but this is not so. He emphasized with scripture how God desires for us to be well and not sick.

Many times I had have neglected to use my power because I believed that power exists only on the outside of me (from a God in a faraway place). I did not know I had power. But this is not so, according to John 4:4 (KJV) "For greater is the power that is within us, than he that is in the world." For many years, I did not understand that verse that was that told to me by my father often. It was not clear to me until I experienced a great tribulation in my life.

What it means to me is that the power to heal is within me. In other words, I already have the power. The greatest power is within my spirit, and that power is the Holy Spirit. I have the power that has already been given to me by God, and this was done through Jesus Christ when He died upon the cross.

We have the power to heal our emotional wounds. Others have attested to this fact, from both a biblical perspective and secular or scientific perspective. Such examples include Andrew Wommack and Dr. Bernie Siegel. Dr. Siegel suggested that our mind (i.e., soul) has the power to heal our bodies if we just listen to spirit which we possess within us.

We are who we be believe ourselves to be and we are who we surround ourselves with. I had to learn that knowledge of who I am was lacking, because if I knew who I was, I would not be seeking power and love outside of myself. This was already given, this is our inheritance.

This is what Ephesians 1:18-19 (NKJV) tells us: "The eyes of your understanding are being enlightened; that you may know what is the hope of his calling, what are riches of the glory of His inheritance in the saints, and what is the exceeding greatness of His power toward us who believe, according to the working of His mighty power." In other words, we have already been given the power by God. We must believe this. For example, a number of successful and prominent people state that the number one factor in personal success in anything is "belief." Many well-known individuals like Oprah Winfrey, Denzel Washington, Will Smith, Sylvester Stallone, Mya Angelou, and Les Brown agree that the key to successful living is the **belief** that your goal can be achieved. Whatever that goal that they were trying to accomplish, belief was present.

The spirit has great power within, but the thing that separates us is the "tapping" in the power of the spirit. This applies to healing our minds, our broken-hearts. We have to take the action and trust the actions will lead to healing. In this case of spiritual perspective, Jesus Christ has already left with this power of healing (Holy Spirit) and instructed on how we should proceed.

This is a thought that came to my mind in 2017, 'Healing is something you do on purpose, something you intend, something you purpose, and something you become. You

become healed and therefore you begin your story as a healer to the masses.'

Telling my story is a termination of my silence and a beginning road to healing. Much of what I am talking about on healing is "universal law"- meaning that this not just my perspective, but it is an understanding that has been proclaimed by individuals from different backgrounds. The bottom line is this: truth is truth.

Researchers on healing, Ventegodt, Andersen, and Merrick (2003), discussed healing from a holistic perspective. They suggest the following: "The holistic process theory explains how this healing comes about: Healing happens in a state of consciousness exactly opposite to the state of crisis. The patient enters the 'holistic state of healing' when (1) the patient and (2) the physician have a perspective in accordance with life, (3) a safe environment, (4) personal resources, (5) the patient has the will to live, (6) the patient and (7) the physician have the intention of healing, (8) the trust of patient in the physician, and (9) sufficient holding." The Scientific World Journal (2003) 3, 1138-1146, Holistic Medicine III: the Holistic Process Theory of Healing.

The key element in the above element is trust, which is simply an indication of **belief** that something will occur as a result of something else.

The above example is from a scientific perspective, however, from a "religious" perspective, the same principles are echoed there must be a **belief** and agreement of healing within the person who is sick and with those providing care, who are praying for them, and who are close to them.

Andrew Wommack speaks on the lessons regarding this when he teaches about the Holy Spirit. As such, Dr. Viktor Frankl's logo therapy, is based on how the human "spirit" remains healthy and untouched even in a time of crisis and pain.

Frankl believed, "Although we can experience sickness in the body and the psyche, the human spirit, our noetic (the intellect) core, remains healthy; however, access to that healthy core can be blocked." The power always remains intact, but is not assessable without belief.

As you continue reading, you will see a story about a woman, named Charity, who you may or may not be familiar to you. This story is narrated throughout this book to provide illustrations of her thought process and her reasoning for her behaviors. Through Charity's story, it is my hope that you will begin to understand her process of healing.

Charity's Story

Her story is being shared to inspire, empower, to give hope, and to encourage others to move toward healing. I desire that this

story may be helpful to others who are suffering in silence from their pain. As you journey with me through her story, you will begin to understand how stepping out of the box of her mind and pressing into God propelled her closer to her destiny and healing.

There was a woman who explained her story in the following manner. She states, "It started with a memory, with a lover that that I had married. It was a marriage that never should have been. Therefore, it had gone bad before it had started. My instinct told me to leave early on, but yet I still returned several times despite the loudness of the spirit telling me otherwise."

She said, "In this memory I remember looking into the eyes of a familiar face, but the eyes were dark and cold as I felt the coldness of his spirit as his massive hands clenched my throat and I thought, Am I going to die!? How did I get to this place?" She continued, "I became numbed, and my mind drifted to another place as his hands tightened around my throat. Perhaps that's what made him stop. My eyes and emotions had grown numb and I was in different place, perhaps in shock."

How did she end up in an abusive marriage? Charity explained that he was deceptive beyond measure, she had been tricked into marrying during her most vulnerable state. She thought that she had waited long enough to get married again (married to her 2nd husband). She thought, "Haven't I studied human nature long enough to avoid such nonsense (abuse)? What was it that led me

14

to be in the company of such abuse?" She sat there in the chair, thinking, "I have not escape the history of my family, where my father abused my mother, and my grandfather was abusive to my grandmother. How did I arrive here? How did I become enraptured with an abuser?"

And this is where she began to investigate herself, behaviors, and familiarities that led her to such a pattern of abusive relationships. She had to start from the beginning to heal.

Charity's Story - Family Cycles and Childhood Experiences

She explains, "I was born in the in the Mississippi Delta and I came from a background of educators, community activists, and entrepreneurs." Much of her journey has been an unexpected one in many senses of the word. She is the youngest child of two within her household. She was extremely close to both her grandmother and mother when she was a young child, around age 7. She could be described as timid, precocious, stubborn, and withdrawn. She was child that was born to premature by weight (4 pounds) although she was a full-term baby. She was the second born with an older sibling.

Her father was smart, witty, charming, but he was also an alcoholic, a womanizer, an abuser, and emotionally broken. Her mother was smart, beautiful, charming, but also broken from abuse, abandonment, and traumatized at a young age. However, nevertheless, this is what she was born into, this was her first learning. Her world became her mother and sister when they moved to another city after her parents' divorce.

When trying to explain herself, she shares some of her parents' background. Her mother was adopted by her great uncle and aunt and raised in the Deep South. She was raised away from her other siblings who remained behind and would soon be scattered among friends and relatives who would take them in.

Her father was 1 of 4 siblings, coming from a family where he was youngest son of specialized technical labor stemming from his father's business. He was raised in the South where oppression plagued the black man and oppression burdened the black woman.

She explained that her father was in world where he felt his voice did not matter, where God was present, but was not evident or acknowledged. There was discontentment. She explained that he was complicated, eccentric, gifted, and discontent, but naturally had a jovial spirit. However, her father was an abuser and womanizer, but that would be oversimplifying the complexity of his being, for he was much greater than that.

Unconsciously, in her mind, from the first man she encountered—her father—she thought that this was the norm in terms of relationships. She describes her family as encountering a "generational curse." There has been a cycle of men from her father's line that follow the same manner of behaviors. It is not an excuse, and it is learned behavior that continued in the generations. For she was birthed into this environment, and has taken her life's course to break the "status quo" normality of this cycle. She became a woman who supported this type of behavior, for this was considered the norm in her mind. Whether she said she believed it or not, her behaviors were the "tell-tale" signs of how she chose her mates and how she interacted with them.

Although others have had similar experiences, her acknowledgment of this was an unconscious belief, which is a belief core which she was not aware of, but played itself out through the her behaviors in her life cycle. She had the belief that you stay and submit in your marriage no matter what, that the husband will grow up in time and stop his philandering, womanizing, gambling or whatever vice he had. That his behavior is only the natural behavior of a 'healthy" male. She was taught to stop overreacting and be a "good woman" because to do otherwise would mean that you are weak, unsupportive, and a little girl who does not know the reality of being a "real woman."

She explained that at the end of her father's life they had become close and he shared the regrets of his actions, and all was forgiven. While he was dying he ruminated how he had lived; and she prayed that he had forgiven himself of his actions. This cycle that confined him was a cycle that she thought she had avoided and had missed. But then, she too became a subject to an abusive man. And this is where her journey toward renewal and destiny began. Out of the pain that she thought she had avoided, it reaped itself into her own life.

Reflections

How can you, by going against the grain of family traditions, change your life? To do so, what do you think would happen?

_____

_____

_____

_____

_____

_____

Charity's Story - Busyness

In the beginning of her life, she described herself as a woman who thought and felt she had to do everything right and be "Ms. Perfect." She thought if she did not do everything right, something terrible would happen.

She explained, "While I was not consciously aware of this problem, this problem existed in my mind. I was not aware that I was indeed worthy, worthy of what I did not yet know." She would soon find out after her many academic, career achievements, and personal challenges, and sometimes what she considered failures (as blessings of teachable moments).

In essence, she did not feel that she was worthy of love. She lived constantly in search of that something to fill that deep dark hole in her soul, but being unable fill it led to frustration, confusion, and finally a spiritual break-down. She thought to herself, "Something has got to give!"

At that point, she came to the crossroads to choose a path that has been there all long, but she'd neglected to follow it fully. This path is the path her Creator was waiting to give her all along. Her Creator was wanting to help her in her struggles, yet she neglected to follow it. Why did she neglect it? Perhaps she lost sight of who God really was or never really understood that unconditional love of God. It could have been unawareness to the voice inside her that was instructing.

Being still was not an option, for she felt she had missed the mark (failing at two marriages). However, it was through her lowest moments, that she began to realize that God had provided a way for her, and that Christ was there to bear all her burdens and sorrows. She also realized that His love and grace was endless, thinking to herself, "God has loved me through all my trials and tribulations even when I did not think He was there. God has always been here with me!"

Thus, in the process of her first divorce, custody battle, graduate school, clinical internship, and a dissertation, she was the workaholic. She went through school and through a number of superficial, unhealthy relationships, without acknowledging the pain she was truly experiencing. She was using the work and sex to self-medicate all her pain, thinking that somehow she would just get over it, and the pain would stop and she would forget about it all. She denied what she wanted and needed because she was afraid of rejection and failure, so she did not try get or ask for more of what she truly wanted. What she really wanted was love and acceptance, saying, "I didn't know God had already accepted me and I was always loved."

Charity was ashamed of being divorced, and felt unworthy of anything better or of anything more because she had failed. Shame was once again preventing the path to healing and her destiny. She confesses to me, "Even to this very day, I have a problems asking for what I want or need." She did not know what it was that she truly wanted. She then realized that she didn't know trying to please others came at the expense of her own happiness.

Her antidote for unhappiness in her mind was having a husband and another child. She thought this was normal and she could blend in, and had learned this from family, friends, and church. No other behavior for a woman was modeled except hard work, commitment to family and marriage, and acceptance of the relationship despite any abuse, and staying in the marriage in the name of forgiveness. Perhaps this was the southern way of cultural socialization among African American women, or maybe she was just caught in a time warp.

The other part of that story was that was that she knew (had knowledge) that abuse was never acceptable. Abuse is an abnormal way of functioning, whether on the receiving end or the giving end. It leads to death of the soul, the emotional, mental state, and sometimes a physical death, when the abuse intensifies.

Although, she learned some good traits like hard work and commitment to family, the concept of balance, faithfulness, reciprocity was missing from the equation. She explains how her **beliefs** (learning) impacted her decisions. Although she believed that abusive behavior was normal, she **knew** instinctively that this was not correct. There is a difference between **knowing** and **belief.**

Charity explained that she did not know who she really was. She did not know her true identity, since she was trying to live up to others' expectations of her. She had to learn her identity. She needed to understand herself and accept her own voice. She needed accept the knowledge of who she was, and not what believed who she was. Charity found these things to be true: "You need to understand who you are and listen to God, through his word in order to better understand your purpose and self-definition. Understanding who you are is an important aspect to guide you in propelling your life's purpose in how you want to live your life."

Reflections

What are some messages that you learned growing up? How have these messages impacted your choices? How do you want live your life, based on the beliefs others have of you or based on the knowledge of self? This question was a hard one for me to answer, and to be honest, I had given it little thought. But the most important question is, what does God want for my life? What is it that God wants for your life?

_____

_____

_____

_____

_____

_____

This is what I now know: I am a woman passionate about starting what she has begun with a great love for my family, and loyalty to no end. However, who I am is not limited to me, it is defined by the purpose that the Lord has within me! I am defined by what I love and what I want to do, for it shows my heart. What

I believe can determine my path and determine what I choose to fight for and who I choose to love.

Many times we define ourselves in terms of the roles we play. However, this is limiting since those roles in life change, disappear, or become null and void as time passes. Therefore, it is important that we do not limit or define ourselves in the sense of the World, the cardinal sense, but from a spiritual perspective, for this is consistent and steady.

If I define myself as a child of God, that is loved, given grace, and is righteous, does that change when I make a mistake? Of course, consequences are always there, but even still, I am loved by the Lord. For example, a woman says, "I am the wife of John, and the mother of three children, an elementary school teacher, and the youth coordinator at church." Although there may be stability in her position in those roles, such as a mother, others are more likely to change over time, such as teacher and youth coordinator. These are the things that she does, this is not who she is. This is not her identity. Her unique contributions and how she plays out these roles reveals who she is by her beliefs, and characteristics that are unique to her own being.

I am talking about this because many times when crisis occurs, it disrupts our lives, and we began to wonder where we now fit. But if we understand the core of our being, who we truly are, and strengths which have allowed us to be resilient in this life, it would be no question what we are to do when crises occur. The stability of God's love is consistent through life's changes. And this is the reason our life experiences have prepared us for it! Your life has prepared you for it! My life has prepared me for it!

What happens when she is no longer the wife, the teacher, the mother, or the youth coordinator—who is she then? What she is doing is describing roles and not who she truly is. When these roles become absent, she feels as if something has been taken from her, she feels lost. She loses herself, because maybe she was already lost and did not know it before the crisis. Perhaps the crisis woke her up! Perhaps she did not know the power of God's love before the crisis.

A crisis is defined as a "decisive or critical moment" according to Merriam Webster's Dictionary. It becomes a personal crisis when there is a loss of identity. Sometimes when people experience a crisis, they are not truly clear on who they are anymore. They become unclear of who they are because of what they once understood as reality or the norm is no longer real.

So this is where the crisis began, because their reality has been altered, their world has been turned upside down. They then began to believe and understand the limitations of control in this life and their thought process shifts. Sometimes it shifts to one of understanding, but many times it shifts to hopelessness, helplessness, and loss. This is referred to as depression (Beck, 1967).

You see, the point is, we are not completely in control, but we are in control of how we react to loss, suffering, pain, and crises. These things are rooted in the very core of your spiritual foundation. But your spiritual foundation must have a proper core in order to survive it all. If your spirit does have the proper core, your mind just needs to listen.

Charity's Story - Reflecting Back

This story of revelation grew out of the struggle of a young woman trying to move on with her life after experiencing a stressful, long, and drawn-out divorce with a person whom she'd married at a young age.

Charity was married to her first husband at a young age. She expressed, "I married at a time when I did not fully understand myself as a person, or what I wanted out of life, or my likes and dislikes. I was simply happy to be with someone who gave me attention, and that attention meant love to me...I only wanted love." Her introvert-ness had in many ways limited her life experiences and kept her sheltered from reality. Her heart was in the right place, meaning she did the right things for the wrong reasons.

She married her first husband because she wanted to please God. In her mind, this was right thing to do, according to her biblically-based beliefs, was to not have sex before marriage. "Since I was already having sex with him, I wanted to make it right, so I married him." Because of this, she rushed into marriage, thinking things would fall into place perfectly. However, she did not understand that rushing into marriage for this reason was wrong. Wow! Patience!

I don't think she had learned her lesson for a long time. She continued school, continued being a mother, a daughter, a sister throughout her ordeal, never letting on to others how much all this was affecting her psychologically, spiritually, and mentally. She was suffering a great deal from PAIN...emotional pain that had not yet begun to heal because she kept it covered. It was not acknowledged. She suffered in silence. She became extremely depressed, because she loose and self-identity that had not yet even been solidified. She eventually divorced her first husband. But now she had pain.

Her pain stemmed from a sense of failure, disappointment, and shame associated with divorce and becoming a single mother. She was concerned how people would see her in the religious community. She distanced herself from her home family and church, for she felt a combination of feelings, anger with God, and shame from church folks. This may not have been necessarily true, but her religious beliefs had emphasized marriage heavily, but the parts that were missing in the teaching is the personal relationship with God and becoming married to God first before anyone could enter into your life in the sacred union of a marriage.

During this time, she noticed that God was showing her different things, challenging her beliefs, and her "why" of doing things.

It seems that support was coming from the most unlikely places. Instead of church and family, support came from mentors, friends, ex in-laws, and professors. She was not walking her journey alone. God was with her. He had great plans for her, but she could not see it.

She began her journey toward finding herself and understanding how to live. For the last 10 years of her life (in that marriage) she only been existing, dying a long, drawn-out miserable living death. While in that marriage, she was existing as the "living dead." Never again did she want to experience that the feeling, that life again. In her mind, it was better to simply die than to live a life so miserable. Sometimes, people are in your life for a season, and it's more about you than the other person.

One of the things she needed to do was forgive herself first, and then forgive her ex-husband. She missed out on one thing during that critical period of 10 years: FORGIVENESS for herself and her ex-husband. Instead she lived out a reality of fear and not of love; was driven by fear and safety in her personal life and not by faith, love, and courage. Love was already there, since it was part of her core, but her first love, love for God, was not fully understood or recognized.

During that time, she began to notice the open doors and all the blessings that she thought were unlikely for a single mother. She was in awe and disbelief because she did not fully understand the depth of God's love for her because she was missing a significant ingredient to her healing – forgiveness.

She would later experience falling further into a deeper crisis of pain later, until that the lesson of forgiveness was learned. Charity explained, "I began to reflect on the flowers from the storm, blooming; one such flower, the birth of my first child. Marriage was my storm that created my flower." She expressed that motherhood was her flower.

Motherhood helped her grow out of her shell in order to heal from her extreme social awkwardness and timidly which allowed the strength that was inside her to shine through. Motherhood helped her grow in strength. It was simply the existence of her daughter which pulled her into her womanhood. It was then that she began to bloom with her gifts!

However, she expressed that she had many challenges, and the challenges were caught up in the bitterness she had toward her ex-husband and anger she had toward her father for not being present, and the stories she heard about her father.

She stated, "I didn't know that the anger I had for my father was coming across to others, particularly men, and at the same time I was choosing men who were unavailable to me, because this was my experience. Their unavailability to me was either emotionally or physically, and when they were available, I became detached and pulled away. I guess this was my defense and my way of staying within my comfort zone."

Reflections

Who do you need to forgive? Do you need to forgive yourself? Have you found it difficult to get past the pain? What is keeping that pain alive and present? What good things have come out of your pain? Have you taken the time

_____

_____

_____

_____

_____

When you feel like there is no time to heal, you're probably not giving yourself time to rest, to think, or to meditate. These behaviors include, working all the time without a vacation, not meditating, not spending time with God, constant busyness, until you are too exhausted to deal with your own problems and issues. When you choose to ignore your own needs, you begin to ignore your instincts and your spirit, to the point where you do not even recognize yourself.

Charity's Story

This is what actually happened to this woman. Charity did not know who she truly was, she had no sense of identity. Then one day, as she walked past a mirror in her bathroom, she caught a glimpse of that person, that person in the mirror and saw herself for the very first time. When she slowly walked back in front of the mirror, she was afraid of what she would see. And to her surprise, she was in complete awe of the reflection staring back at her! She thought to herself, "Who is this person? That person in the reflection is beautiful!"

The inner glow reflecting back was like an introduction to self, someone perhaps she had never seen, or simply ignored, faded into the background. This was her reality at some point in her life to fade into background, to have no voice, to not be seen. Because after all, she felt she was an unimportant, insignificant part of environment. It was apparent that she had internalized this thought process into her being, for this was how she related with her family, and perhaps it was also how she chose her mates and other relationships in her life.

Reflections

How many people do you think have experienced this? Have you experienced this? Have you discouraged yourself by telling yourself that you are not worthy, that you're unable to do something or become something? Was it by mistake or on purpose? Take time to reflect on this experience. What were you doing when it happened? Where did the feelings come from?

_____

_____

_____

_____

_____

HEALING DEFINED

"He healed the broken in heart, and bindeth up their wounds."
Psalms 147:3 (KJV)

Healing—what is it? And how do we do it? How do we know we need it? Sometimes we may actually think that we are okay, but are emotionally and spiritually sick. According to Webster's Dictionary, "heal" means to "to make or become sound or whole." Wow, there is a lot of meaning in that one word. So basically, when one acknowledges that she or he needs healing, they are acknowledging that they are broken or not whole in some shape or form.

Let us examine this further. What does it mean to be "whole"? This is important, because in order to heal or become whole, we need to understand what that looks like or what that means. Webster's Dictionary defines the word "whole" as an adjective:

1: being in healthy or sound condition.

2: having all its parts or elements

3: constituting the total sum of;

Or as a noun:

1: complete amount or sum

2: something whole or entire—as in "on the whole"

Ok, I think that clarified everything for us. Well, sort of. Let's back up and slow down to our original question: Healing—what is it? To make or become SOUND or WHOLE.

In essence, to be in the process of healing implies that we are broken in some way that we are NOT whole. In order to heal, we must first acknowledge that brokenness that is affecting us at that very moment.

Healing involves the process of putting the pieces back together. How does God see us? Does He see us in our brokenness? Does God even see us as broken? Does God see in us in way that we see ourselves when we are in despair, hurt, sorrowful, disappointed, and broken-hearted?

God does not see us as broken. God sees us as who we truly are because He has the power of restoration. We become broken in our souls (as in heart-broken or disappointed) or in our bodies (a broken limb, a serious disease, chronic illness), but our spirit is never broken.

Let's recap. When I refer to the soul, I am referring to the mind. When I refer to the body, I am referring to the physical body. When I make reference to the Spirit, I am referring to part of us that we are born with, the part from God. We are not God, but God is within us, in us all the time. You see, if we would only acknowledge his presence, we have the power within us to heal if we understand who we are. We must surrender.

If we acknowledge and understand that our brokenness is part of growth, and that it is our path to something greater; we can embrace the power that is given to us by our Creator. Many distractions in our world keeps us separated from God who is within us. Many times we allow our souls to guide and lead our path while we become deaf to that internal spirit. In short, our path to becoming greater has to do with the spirit that is within us.

Since **acknowledging** is a key component to healing, we must ask ourselves, "What is the problem?" My struggle involved realizing that I was part of problem in my brokenness. It was me not understanding that I was good enough where I was; and good enough in who I was. I thought I was all alone, that I was okay all by myself.

Being alone was illusion that was in my mind because truly, I was never alone. I had family, friends, people who helped, loved, and those admired me whom I did not even know.

You see, God was always there waiting for me call upon Him, to ask him for guidance. I had come to realize that God loved me so much, that guidance was given to me by the Holy Spirit, even when I did not ask, even when I ignored the loud voice of the Holy Spirit saying, "don't do it, go the other way."

Even when I ignored the spirit within me, and did not truly understand the love of God. I was still protected in the midst of fire, even untouched by the fire like Daniel. It was God's grace that saved me and kept in safety, solace, and unharmed by the fire.

In the Bible, in the book of Daniel (3:11-14), there was a king named Nebuchadnezzar who commanded that everyone should fall down and worship his gods, and whoever refused would be cast into a burning fiery furnace. There were three men who worshipped the God of Abraham: Shadrach, Meshach, and Abednego, who refused to fall down and worship the king's god of the golden image. And for this offense, the king had them punished and sentenced to death by throwing them into a fiery furnace.

However, these three men were protected in the mist of the fire. The son of God was in their midst. They surrendered to will of God and did not worship false gods. Even in the fire, they were protected and untouched (see Daniel 3:26-27, AMPC).

Then Nebuchadnezzar the king [saw and] was astounded, and he jumped up and said to his counselors, 'Did we not cast three men bound into the midst of the fire?' They answered, 'True, O King.' He answered, 'Behold, I see four men loose,

walking in the midst of the fire, and they are not hurt! And the form of the fourth is like a son of the gods!' Then Nebuchadnezzar came near to the mouth of the burning fiery furnace and said, 'Shadrach, Meshach, and Abednego, you servants of the Most High God, come out and come here.' Then Shadrach, Meshach, and Abednego came out from the midst of the fire. And the satraps, the deputies, the governors, and the king's counselors gathered around together and saw these men–which the fire had no power upon their bodies, nor was the hair of their head singed; neither were their garments scorched or changed in color or condition, nor had even the smell of smoke clung to them."

You see even we are condemned and thrown in the "fire" by people, it important that we stay faithful to God. God loves us despite our faults and will protects. He wants us to trust His strength in our weakness. God protects us in the midst of obedience- He is our protector. God protected the Woman while she was going through the "fiery furnace" of her trials of loss, abuse, and disappointment- she was being shielded even when she did not know it, she was covered.

Charity's Story

She talked about how doubting her own instinct lead to destructive decisions; how fear prevented her from breaking free of bad situations or sharing her pain, depression, and brokenness. She entered a situation here she ran right into arms of another broken person, a predatory being, who preyed on her brokenness, but even then, he did not know God was protecting her in the fire.

God was protecting her from her enemy, even though she was would sleeping with her enemy who became her husband, against all good reason, and spiritual warning. Yes, there was warning, but her mind has ignored the ever so small voice of the spirit. She thought it was only her mind, because she had not been taught about the spirit that which was within her. After overcoming so much trauma, pain and disappointment, she began to acknowledge that it was only God that had delivered her. She explained that she relied on the scripture, Psalm 23 to remind her of God's grace, love, and power.

She believed, "God has always promised to protect us from those who wish to deceive and harm us. God will never forsake us; He is our armor and shield at all times, and in His presence we are protected and His presence is always with us."

Psalms 23 describes this beautifully:

"The LORD is my shepherd; I shall not want. He makes me to lie down in green pastures; He leads me beside the still waters. He restores my soul; He leads me in the paths of righteousness For His name's sake. Yea, though I walk through the valley of the shadow of death, I will fear no evil; for You are with me; Your rod and Your staff, they comfort me. You prepare a table before me in the presence of my enemies; You anoint my head with oil; My cup runs over. Surely goodness and mercy shall follow me All the days of my life; And I will dwell in the house of the LORD Forever." Psalms 23:1-6(NKJV)

This scripture reminds me of the protection of God. When reflecting on Charity's story, I began to witness it in my daily life in small reminders. I heard a pastor talking about protection in a story by an unknown person. Many times we are protected and we do not know even know why or how. Sometimes we ask and call on help, not really believing it will come, but when it comes, we recognize it as a miracle.

There was miracle regarding a man who was in the midst of war. It is stated that he was running from the enemy and he found a cave and he went into one of the caves. While he was in the cave he prayed fervently to God to please spare his life and to protect him from the enemy. At the very moment a spider came down from above and began to spin a web up quickly over the cave over the cave's opening. At the very moment the enemy began approaching and began to search the various caves, however when they came to his cave they decided not to search his cave because they said, surely with that web, it would have been disturbed, so they overlooked his cave and the man was protected (Author Unknown).

The story illustrates how God is always protecting you and how His way is not always our way. The man thought so little of the spider, and did not know how spider would protect him, but God knew that the cave would be overlooked when a web was in spun in front of it.

I heard this story when I was concerned about protection. I heard this story during a television broadcast where the pastor was talking about a man who was praying for protection in the midst of war. Prior to hearing that story, I was feeling down and discouraged. That story gave me hope, where I learned that the Lord will always protect you when you ask for it.

Later on that same day, as my heart was heavy, I went to work out at the gym, and while I was exercising on the elliptical, there appeared a spider spinning a web in front of me. This was an odd place to see a spider, but it was reminder of the story I had just heard about protection. At that moment, I was comforted because I knew that God was protecting me. At the front door of my home, there was also a prominent large spider that spun a web there;

and there were spider webs on each window in the back yard of new home, with large webs to cover each window. A coincidence, maybe, maybe not!

Charity's Story -Death and Loss

Charity explained that after dealing with so much death and disappointment in the year 2014, she was not in the right mind to make a decision. She had lost several family members: an aunt, uncle, a 17-year-old close family friend, a 39-year-old family friend, and other family members on her mother's and stepfather's side—all while serving as the caregiver for her sick biological father. In the midst of not dealing her own grief, she masked her pain with things and pleasure, trying to medicate the pain. This resulted in her becoming deeply involved with the wrong man.

She stated that in retrospect that was no time be entertaining a relationship with anyone. She was too vulnerable to be in her right mind to make a sound decision about one's character, financial decisions, or even entertain marriage. She felt that she was alone. She had no voice of reason, since she had isolated herself and restrained herself from hearing anyone or anything who could help. She was SILENT in her own pain which she was experiencing prior to her second marriage. She was right where the enemy wanted her to be—vulnerable, isolated, and without the presence of wise counsel. But GOD protected her even still so that no harm would prevail. This takes me back to understanding the power of God's hand in healing us.

After three miscarriages and a loss of thousands in investments, in a false loveless marriage of one year, she now understood that God was her protecting in the midst of fire.

As her sister would tell her all the time in consolation, "God only wants your highest good." She contemplated and talked about all the ways in which the Holy Spirit interceded to warn and protect her; and all the time she was trusting in man and not God. But she gave it to God and things fell into place as they should. God is still with her.

Earlier, she began to wonder, thinking, "Is God punishing me? Have I done something wrong? Why are there so many complications in my leaving my ex-husband (second marriage) when the previous times were easier and so less complicated? I left because I believed that he had been unfaithful, and I stayed gone because he was so verbally abusive towards me. However, I foolishly returned when he came with a long drawn out apology with promises of change- it was all an act. Why did I not trust my instinct to leave the first time as correct and just stick to it? Was it because I was listening to people instead of God? Wow, I left 3 times and the 3rd time was my last!"

Her ability to leave physically was so easy, but that spiritual departure was the most difficult for her. She did not understand her worth, value, and the treasure and gift that God saw in her. This was something that she did not understand until it became struggle became more difficult. It was only then did she fight; she was lukewarm at first. She knew that she had made a mistake by depending on the validation of others when God had already given her the answers. She explained this to me: "We see how quickly things can change when we try to do things in our own power and not by through the power of God's guidance. There are disastrous results when we don't include God. This speaks to our lack of wisdom and frailty without God. But with God, the redeemer of all can redeem all that you thought you had lost because it has drawn you closer to God and his will."

She stated, "My instinct was telling me leave and not go back for a 2nd time to go back my husband. But I doubted my instincts, and dismissed the inkling to leave as only fear." She eventually realized, that "fear is not a bad thing, this "fear" was simply something within my spirit, telling me that I am on dangerous ground, I'm walking in unholy territory."

She explained that God was giving her the insight; however, she dismissed it. You know that there is always a reason—the death of friends or family, the stress and grief of caring for her father and ultimately planning for his funeral. It was too much bear, or so it seemed, but God was there.

When looking back, she understood that she was not herself. She was broken and wanted desperately to find some happiness, some newness, in all her of my sadness. She did not want to deal with the grief.

She thinks that she was allowed to go through struggle, not for herself, but for maybe for her ex-husband was this more for him than for her. She explained, "But of course, all good things come from above. Any bad thing that we experience comes not from God, but God can create something beautiful from our mess."

It seemed that everything was forced: her dating process, the marriage, and the coming together.

Something just did not seem to quite right. She did not listen to her inner voice, but instead looked to others to validate or invalidate her thoughts and beliefs. She believed what others were saying over her inner voice (instinct).

She was challenging others without looking at herself and her challenges, her desire to control and make everything "right." Thus, her happiness depended on someone else's ability to live up to what she wanted, or simply put, to do what she wanted.

In psychology, we call this **co-dependency**. And she wandered to herself, "Why did I get involved in relationships with those people who are addicted one thing or another—drugs, sex, or gambling?"

She realized that she was depending on him to feel better, depending on a man and not God. She stated, "This was my downfall."

Reflections

Have you ever been in a situation where you were unsure of what to do? Have you been so unsure that you sought counsel? Did you know who to seek? Did you hear the Holy Spirit speaking to you, gently guiding you? Were you still long enough to even get an answer? Do you remember being protected by God?

_____

_____

_____

_____

Charity's Story (Background)

Unfortunately, she learned that change comes with age and illness, sometimes bitterness settles in on the others heart. She learned that it was important to stick by your man no matter what, and that time and forgiveness would be the glue that would resist brokenness. Once such instance of this, is when she sat in the kitchen during a discussion about relationships and marriage. Listening, she heard a woman say, 'you either are going to be with him or not, if you don't want him don't play games.' Charity sat there silently, taking it all in, "Thinking I have to make a commitment even if I am not sure...but I made a mistake, I was tricked into this one, I gave my loyalty to wrong man and now I have to figure out how to get myself out."

Charity explained, "I thought it was my responsibility to keep the family together, and the man would eventually catch up. I stopped dreaming, painting, exercising, and sacrifice my life for a man and children that cared nothing about me. I know understand how I got myself into that situation, I thought that this was the way marriage was done." What she learned in relationships is that woman sacrifice most things, if not everything. And that she must give up part of herself to make the relationship work. Now this is in no way saying that one person is the blame for another's behavior, however, how we choose who we "love" has more to do with our own experiences. What we know, what we believe to be true, and what we believe is our reality.

Reflections

How can we get past our generational patterns or family traditions? How do can you get a different outcome than your past? Think about several events that impacted your present life over 3 days. Write down the event and the impacts of that event in another row. Are your generational patterns keeping you from healing or coming into your purpose?

_____

_____

_____

_____

_____

_____

Guilt and Shame

While listening to a sermon, a pastor discussed how shame and guilt keeps us from our destiny. He was teaching about the difference between shame and guilt during a church service which I attended for the very first time. The pastor explained how having "shame" prevents healing and how shame and guilt are different.

He stated that, Shame as, "I am sorry for who I am" and Guilt is, "I am sorry for what I did." And up until that time, I perceived shame and guilt to be one in the same meaning. He further explained that Shame involves the feelings of inadequacy, of feeling that "I'm not enough." And that this feeling of inadequacy (not good enough) is what keep us from healing, it's what keeps us from reaching our destiny.

The pastor went on to give an example of this matter in the Bible when Saul was destined and was appointed king, but because of his feelings of inadequacy, he felt shame and ran away. He did not done anything wrong-guilt, but he felt shame.

In I Samuel 9:21, it is written, **"Saul replied, 'But I'm only from the tribe of Benjamin, the smallest tribe in Israel, and my family is the least important of all the families of that tribe! Why are you talking like this to me?'"**

This was message for those who deny themselves what God has given them all because of fear, of feeling that they are not good enough. However, on the other hand, David made some bad choices regarding Bathsheba, which led to dire consequences for others and eventually himself. However, David dealt with his shame in a different way.

In the story (II Samuel 11, 12), King David laid with a servant's wife and she conceived. David then had the servant husband killed purposefully at war; then David took the servant's wife Bathsheba and made her his wife and she bore him a son. Because this displeased God, the child died even after David had pleaded and fasted with God.

David had to endure the consequence of his evil acts. In Psalms 51:14, David presented a sense of guilt in his prayer to the Lord, when he says, "Deliver me from guilt of bloodshed, O God, the God of my salvation, and my tongue shall sing aloud of your righteousness."

Guilt

As stated earlier, guilt is something that you are sorry for doing. It is an action. However, shame is the feeling that that you have about that action, which you attribute to yourself.

Guilt is by definition as a noun: "The fact of having committed a specified or implied offense or crime; bad feeling caused by knowing or thinking that you have done something bad or wrong; or the state of one who has committed an offense, especially consciously; b) feelings of culpability, especially for imagined offenses or from a sense of inadequacy."

Thus, some have noted that **guilt** is synonymous with **shame.** This issue of guilt and shame is presented here because these are some emotions which an individual may experience when they encounter a trauma, major life change, or some other bad actions that comes about in life.

With shame, there is possibility of experiencing feelings of guilt, regret or embarrassment. But is it not for us to stay in this place, because this staying here, it stifles us, stops our growth, makes us sick, and creates a domino effect of negativity on our lives.

Yes, we are to acknowledge the feelings as they come, acknowledge that pain when it is there, when it happens, but we cannot stay there by any means. For this blocks our healing and our destiny. Though it is a cliché to say, "When one door closes another door opens." But this true, and we must be willing to walk through that door. If we stay in that place of shame or guilt, we channel our energy in a negative place. We become depressed and anxious about life.

Reflections

Why do many feel shame or guilt when they go through a stressful situation, make a mistake, take chances (and fail), when thing don't go as they expected or plan? Where does this come from? Do you feel shame and guilt when you go through a traumatic or stressful situation? If so, why?

_____

_____

_____

_____

_____

_____

Charity's Story - Flashback

Charity looked at how doubting her own instinct led to destructive decisions; how fear prevented her from breaking free of bad situations or sharing her pain, depression, and brokenness. She started to date this man whom she said she would never date. Her spirit told her all the things he was from the very beginning, and they were all correct.

When they were "friends," meaning nothing sexual, no closeness, not even a hug or deep two-way conversations, he labeled the discourse as a friendship. Although his was no friendship from her perspective. She was a people-pleaser, so she went with the flow to the point of lying to herself. She prided herself in being a friend to another and being loved by another was paramount.

However, he was being deceptive and it was a friendship only as long as he could get his way. He was self-centered and narcissistic to say the least. Charity explained that all his conversations were one-sided, were told from his perspective, and when you had an opinion, he would criticize you heavily for your opinions. Or when you told him about your life, he would criticize or belittle you for your actions when there was a mistake on your part.

This person was absent for 2 years of her life because she had cut all communication with him, because of a verbal offenses he had made. They only reconnected in error after she had encountered life changing and traumatic event in her life which included betrayal and shock from someone she had trusted and thought was a friend.

Charity had been going through number of trials including the death of several family members and the failing health of father who diagnosed with cancer at his later stages. All at the same time dealing with a spiritual battle of relationship with God and what she believed and what she wanted. After several failed relationships, and wanting companionship, there seemed to be one bad mistake after other. This led to offenses against herself by others, all in the name of "giving the benefit of the doubt" when her spirit and discernment would be telling her otherwise.

She thinks regretfully that had she listened to her spirit, she would not have suffered what she had lost. She sat there, crying silently, asking herself, "What did I do to get here? " But yet, God's grace was sufficient and she was covered and protected, even still. What came out this trauma was spiritual renewal and integration into her destiny which God had given to her. She had been given a spiritual BIRTH of her purpose and destiny on this earth. God redeemed all time and loss!

She explained, "The Spirit is always there to help you if you just listen; deceit is all around us, but what we need is truth and not charm.... For charm is deceit wrapped in a pretty ribbon, and means you no good, but only harm."

When turmoil was going on her life, she reached for something, somebody's to help her numb the pain of her losses and wanted to feel happy about something once again. She did the routine instead of using that time alone to be comforted by power within her, the Holy Spirit. The mind is powerful because it reaches for the familiar and her familiar was not good. And then this broken person latched on to her because he saw an opportunity to improve things in his life. She was only an opportunity to him which he pursued fervently.

If she had not been in the midst of pain, vulnerable, and if she had understood whose she was, she would have recognized who he really was and his true motives as she did the first time she met him. She was, at that time, grasping for a lifeline that she thought he was. She explains, "In retrospect, he was using me as a lifeline in his emptiness, during my crisis." When all she needed was GOD, He was there all the time and was the only lifeline she needed, for God is the creator and supplier of all things good.

She had in many ways become numbed to her senses. Trauma and grief has a way of numbing you, of deafening your ears, and blinding your vision, numbing your feelings, desensitizing your instincts to what is TRUTH. With this numbing, it is difficult to distinguish between fear and intuition. You cannot hear what the spirit is telling you. You are like a walking dead person, existing in the shell of the body, though physically alive. This is what trauma does to you. It desensitizes you to the abnormal - so when trauma continues, your threshold of what you can accept becomes higher; whereas the "normal" or non-traumatized person recognizes bad, unpleasant things for what they are immediately and responds accordingly.

All of that was said to explain how deception covered and attacked while she was dead in her senses from grief and trauma from the loss of her father and 10 other family members and friends over that past year. And this is where the end of her journey begins. With this, she begins to see the greatness of God and understands what she has gone through in her second marriage—the abuse, deep deceit, sickness—only to be propelled closer to God. She realized that God had pulled her out of something so deep, that only He could have done it! And with this, she had to overcome her shame of being in that situation and begin her journey to healing.

Shame

According to the Merriam Webster Dictionary, the definition of Shame is as follows:

1. A painful emotion caused by consciousness of guilt, shortcoming or impropriety;

2. A condition of humiliating disgrace or disrepute;

3. Something that brings censor or reproach; or

4. Something to be regretted.

Synonyms: regret, remorse, repentance, contrite, penitence, self-reproach, guilt.

However, for the purposes of understanding we will go the pastor's definition of shame (refer to the story of Saul explained earlier) including "feelings of inadequacy."

It's like that person has internalized the act into who they are, but they are not the act. So because the mistake or action was bad, they believe that they too must be bad.

All in all, many have experienced the feeling of shame at some point in their lives. So the question is: what do we do with that shame? How do we move forward from regrets, remorse, disgrace, shortcomings? To move from shame involves acts of forgiveness and grace.

In life circumstances, when you feel a sense of shame, you feel as if everyone is against you and that you deserve it, however, God does not want us to stay in this place. In life, shame can make you feel like this. It can make you feel depressed and hopeless about any future.

Sometimes when you feel down and want cry, there is a feeling that there is no time to cry, to speak, to express, or heal. You feel that you're only supposed to keep moving.

For example, when I reached for some comfort, because I was feeling down, I began to have negative thoughts: Why is God punishing me? Why am I such a bad person? Do I deserve this?

I was feeling bad and blaming God.

Why do we feel shame? Why does our shame persist? Is it that we have allowed ourselves to believe that others can judge us or that we are not worthy of forgiveness?

For example, the woman who has been in an abusive relationship. Others would judge her and say, "She allowed the abuse, she allowed the beatings." In essence they are saying she deserved it, without saying it, they have judged her harshly, the victim, the 'would be' survivor of the abuse. But how is her abuse perpetuated?

Therefore, she goes from day to day in silence not reaching out for help, but suffering in silence; putting on a mask of "I'm okay." She internalizes this thought: "It was something wrong that I did to cause that anger or to cause that behavior" or believing "I have no other way to live" or believing that "time will bring change." In essence, she doesn't reach out, because she begins to feel that she is to blame and her SILENCE is great and perpetual!

For her offspring becomes a witness to these behaviors and these become the "normative" behavior for relationships. It becomes a perpetual cycle of dysfunction.

I asked myself, "Why do we live in a world that makes the victim the enemy; we live in a world that makes the victim ashamed, where wickedness is rewarded and righteousness is look down upon."

This is a fallen world. However, this is not the ending, but the beginning of this story, there is hope, for those who survive, learn to forgive themselves for what was placed upon them during life, or for what they have placed upon themselves.

I think about Psalm 91:2-3, which encourages me to persist in the Lord, stay in faith. **"I will say of the Lord, He is my refuge and fortress: my God; in Him I will trust. Surely he shall deliver thee from the snare of the fowler, and from the noisome pestilence."**

Reflections

What has shame made you hide? What has shame stopped you from doing? How have you stopped living? What has shame stopped you from doing? How has shame kept you from healing? List ways you believe shame has withheld you from your destiny.

_____

_____

_____

_____

_____

_____

Forgiveness

What is forgiveness? It is a pardon, or allowing room for error or weakness (Merriam Webster Dictionary).

According an article from The Greater Good Foundation of UC Berkley, it is suggested that psychologist define forgiveness as: "a conscious deliberate decision to release feelings of resentment or vengeance toward a person or a group who has harmed you, regardless of whether they actually deserved your forgiveness."

Additionally, it was also noted that forgiveness does not equal reconciliation; "it does not obligate you to reconcile with the person who harmed you, or release them from legal accountability." But rather forgiveness, "brings peace of mind" and frees that individual from "corrosive anger." Retrieved on September 5, 2018, from

https://greatergood.berkeley.edu/topic/forgiveness/definition.

Throughout the Bible, there are many demonstrated acts of forgiveness. Jesus Christ performed acts of forgiveness. His acts were motivated by the love of God, performed as an example to teach us about love. The love of God is why Jesus was sacrificed and died upon the cross for the remission of our sins, whether we deserve forgiveness or not, which we don't.

You may ask why there is a section in this dedicated to forgiveness. I have mentioned forgiveness several times throughout this book because forgiveness is an important aspect of healing. This has been always been the case; healing was not meant to be separate from forgiveness. For Jesus came not to condemn the world, but to give salvation.

Jesus' purpose here was to teach us to love, to trust in Him, and heal to those who are broken. He came to heal and restore; and restoration cannot be accomplished without forgiveness. For restoration is part of healing. Therefore, a large part of healing is forgiveness, forgiveness of self and others.

Forgiveness allows us to heal, which allows us to move forward. It is difficult to move forward briskly while looking back. Un-forgiveness makes progress slow and unproductive. But when you only look forward to your future, you are building strength toward positivity. That is one of the reasons I knew I had to forgive, not for others but as a gift to myself. I needed to stop denying the pain, the bitterness, and the lack. When we hold on to bitterness in our hearts because of something that was done to us or someone else, we harbor those emotions, and miss the mark or block opportunities for new relationships or new beginnings.

This is demonstrated in Matthew 18: 21-35, in the parable of the unforgiving servant. In a brief explanation, the Servant had debt to the king, and the master of that servant had forgiven and released him of his debt. However, later, that same servant, did not forgive another who owed him!

In Matthew 18:29-34 (NKJV), it states: "So his fellow servant who fell at his feet and begged him, saying, 'Have patience with me, and I will pay you all.' And he would not, but went and threw him into prison till he should pay his debt. So when his fellow servants saw what had been done, they were very grieved, and came and told their master, after he had called him, said to him,

"You wicked servant! I forgave you all that debt because you begged me. Should you not also have had compassion on your fellow servant, just as I had pity on you? And his master was angry, and delivered him to the torturers until he should pay all that was due him."

God forgives us daily of our sins, the sins we acknowledge and the sins we do not know about. Jesus Christ died for the remission of our sins; he was our sacrifice. The question is, how is it that we have been so forgiven, have gained this gift of forgiveness, but hardened our hearts when comes to others? Christ came to provide salvation and not condemnation, but we take it take it upon ourselves to condemn regularly, in the form of complaining, bitterness, envy, revenge, etc. We do this in form of condemnation out of fear, and not love.

Without love, there is no compassion, no forgiveness, and ultimately no healing.

Forgiveness is the pathway to healing. It is the "Medicine" for a wound that festered, in the midst of un-forgiveness. And the only one who ends up suffering is the one who does not forgive. The Bible teaches many lessons about forgiveness, how to forgive, and why we should forgive. For many years I did not understand how my un-forgiveness was blocking my progress and my healing. Un-forgiveness, in short, keeps us in despair. It kept me in despair for many years, and I did not even know it. For God has shown us how to forgive in His Word. In Psalms 130:7 (NKJV) it states: "O Israel, hope in Lord for with the Lord there is mercy, and with Him is abundant redemption."

In the Bible, the book of Psalm provides us with an example of how our God forgives through His grace and mercy, and how through His forgiveness there is healing of our iniquities (sins). God only wants us healed, but we must be willing to receive. I needed to receive it and ask for it. I only needed to believe that God is a God of abundance and grace and has the power to heal me.

Forgiveness is a part of healing, and one cannot one truly heal without forgiveness. In the Bible, I would read how often forgiveness and healing go hand in hand. Another example, was 2 Chronicles 7:14; "**Then if my people who are called by my name will humble themselves and pray and seek my face and turn from their wicked ways, I will hear from heaven and will forgive their sins and restore their land."**

Here it shows how God both acted in forgiveness and healing (restoration). It shows us such an example of these two concepts, how individuals are forgiven despite their actions. What I did not understand is that forgiveness also includes forgiving yourself. It involves forgiving yourself for bad decisions, for missed opportunities, for mediocrity, or for whatever you have done that you have not YET forgiven yourself for.

It is not just about forgiving the other person. In order to fully reconcile, renew self and heal, you MUST also forgive yourself! It is your mindset in how you must proceed, it is a renewing and transformation of your mind.

This is my prayer, "Dear God, I ask that you forgive all those who have done me wrong with or without intention. Dear God, teach them and forgive them, allow me to accept a spirit of change and penitence through your word, O Dear Lord, in Jesus name. Amen."

Fear vs. Instinct – How do you know the difference?

Fear is something that most of us are acquainted with. Fear is an issue I became acquainted with during many points in my life. What is fear? It's an unpleasant emotion caused by the belief that someone or something is dangerous, likely to cause pain, or a threat.

According to Merriam Webster Dictionary, Fear is "an unpleasant, often strong emotion caused by anticipation or awareness of danger." But are all fears based in reality? Are some fears simply anxiety, ideas that we make up in our mind that are not necessarily true?

I am sure many people have been faced with fear at one point in their life. Am I fearing failure or success? You see, I have done things in my life, one of which I felt that was a failure because of a failed relationship. I have made some destructive decisions, because of fear; and I have made some dangerous choices because I ignored my instinct. It is important to know the difference between the two—*fear* and *instinct*—otherwise you could be placed on the wrong path.

I took a leap into dangerous and destructive territory when I got the two confused. But I will reveal more about that later, and you will understand this application. I was in dangerous territory, all the while ignoring the voice of God, my instincts, ignoring the signs that God was bringing forth to me. I simply dismissed it as fear. I was deceived and clarity was not with me.

But not all fear is bad, once you understand the context, the purpose, and then it's NOT fear, but it is instinct, it is intuition, it is the Holy Spirit warning you!

You must able to discern the difference between FEAR and protection in the form of intuition, instinct, Holy Spirit.

I feared being alone, but the whole time I was never alone; GOD was with me. God was protecting me in the midst of fire, in the midst of evil, in the midst of deceit. I was protected, despite my decisions, my mistakes, and God's grace was forever present. My fear overrode my instinct. I could not hear!

That was the point in my life where I could not determine the difference between the two: fear or instinct. I lacked clarity on what I was supposed to pay attention to. Here is what I now know, fear is something irrational, something that you're afraid of that could happen. Instinct was telling me what was in the present moment, what my truth of what the situation was. It was not a guess, but it was something definite, something that I felt in depth of my gut.

Instinct was the gut-wrenching feeling that the more I went against the instinct, the sicker I felt. My decisions went against my instinct, therefore proceeded with substantial disease until I muted my instincts to the point of muting my own voice, yes muting my own internal voice. My lack of confidence drove me to seek out validation from external factors, to validate what my instincts were telling me, and all the time those external factors negated my internal my instinct, and dismissed them simply as "fear."

Therefore, in looking back I can cannot blame my external factors (family, friends) for my decisions, but only blame the lack of clarity and confidence knowing and living my own truth. I have learned that instincts are powerful internal factors that we should listen to and propel our life to our definitive destiny!

In life we have many things that we fear. But we must learn to listen to what fear is telling us about the situation. Is it telling us to pay attention to something, go in another direction, or proceed?

That is why we should listen to the source of our fear: is the source rooted in success (fear of success), failure (fear of failure), inadequacy (fear that you are not enough or are not good enough), or in danger?

In the realm of fear of success, this fear should be your guide to proceed. This is where we should proceed with the task in spite of your fear, for this is courage. For courage is proceeding despite your fear. This faith that God will cover you toward your destiny! God is our greatest "fear killer." The reason I say this is because God never leaves us, He is always there.

In Deuteronomy 31:8 (NKJV), it states, "And the Lord, he is the One who goes before you. He will be with you, and He will not leave you nor forsake you; do not fear or be dismayed."

Reflections

Food for thought: Your mindset has much to do with whether you change or remain stagnant. How will you ever know if you don't take the leap? Can we fully live and receive all our blessings if we live in fear? What are some things your instinct has instructed to do but you have not move on it because of fear?

_____

_____

_____

_____

_____

FACTORS PREVENTING HEALING

Words

Words are powerful! Words can make or break a relationship. What we believe in our minds comes out in our words. Our minds reflect our hearts which manifest through our speech.

My great uncle would always tell me, "Think twice, and speak once," which is an old saying that many would use.

This is something I noticed in my life, that there are those individuals who know exactly what to say in any given circumstance and are able to better maneuver through situations, than those who tend to bark out words and phrases with no thought of consequences.

Many times our words reflect our own fears and insecurities. These are distractions from blessings. With all the different emotions we experience, our words can destroy people and opportunities if we are wise. It is an ongoing learning process to allow our words to serve as a creative force in the universe.

Because words are a reflection of our thoughts, it is important to be aware of what we focus on, what we listen to, and what we feed ourselves mentally. We need to be conscious and intentional of our spiritual and mental diet. For many times we do not protect our minds from negative thoughts, negative stimuli.

I remember when I was trying to stay positive. I noticed that there were so many opportunities to become negative. I had to become intentional about what I allowed into my mind. We are constantly surrounded with negative media, television, internet, smart phones, and people we are closest to at times.

This has been a problem, the misuse of words, since the beginning of time. Proverbs 4:23-24 KJV speaks to this issue of words:

"Keep thy heart with all diligence; for out of it are the issues of life"; Put away from thee a forward mouth, and perverse lips, put far from thee."

When looking at the same verse from GW (God's Word) translation; Verse 4:23-24 it states: "Guard your hearts more than anything else because the source of your life flows from it. Remove dishonesty from your mouth. Put deceptive speech far away from your lips." That explains how our words could uplift or bring down individuals, circumstances, etc. There is power in words. The old saying, "Sticks and stones may break my bones, but words will never hurt" is such a fallacy and could not be further away from the truth.

Another way of putting this is that our words reflect our own hearts, mind, and what we are truly feeling. It's important that we are careful of what goes into our minds. If we think we are a failure, thinking, "I will never pass this class," or "I will never advance at my job because my boss does not like me," or "he will never marry me," or "I will never marry" or that we are stupid incompetent, unworthy—we will act accordingly even when we try not to. It goes like the following:

→ THINKING → CREATES ACTION→ CREATES MOTION→MOTIVATIONS

Our belief creates our reality and actions. In the book of Proverbs, it states:

"For as he thinketh in his heart, so is he, eat and drink, saith he to thee; but his heart is not with thee. The morsel which thou hast eaten shalt vomit up, and lose thy sweet words."

Specifically, this verse is stating that what you place in your mind comes back out of your mouth. Another such example is cited in Proverbs 18:21 (KJV):

"Death and life are in the power of the tongue: and they that that love it shall eat the fruit thereof."

With this understanding, in hearing and reading the word of God, it was clear to me that I must be careful of my words, for I am for I am dictating my future.

This was a message that has stayed on my mind for days, and one that I am careful to be aware of in my daily actions.

You are what you believe, and you are what you say; the tongue reflects the inner self!

Busyness

"For I know the plans I have for you," says the Lord, "They are plans for good and not for disaster, to give you a future and a hope." Jeremiah 29:11 (NKJV)

Sometimes we are not still enough to hear God and his plans for our lives because we are in constant busyness. Is busyness blocking your healing? The definition of busyness "is the state of having a lot of activity, or of not being idle. When you have a lot of tasks to do all at once, this is an example of busyness."

The lies of busyness includes the idea that "I cannot stop and rest because I too much to do." The stories we tell ourselves to justify our busyness! What is it that are we running from?

When I speak with individuals who suffer from trauma, they often tell me that they try to stay busy all the time. They tell me that they try to stay busy to avoid thinking about the trauma they experienced or witnessed. People sometimes stay busy to help get through the day, to ignore the past painful events. But then they also say that they have trouble sleeping at night, have problems with relationships, and have problems with concentration, have problems enjoying everyday things in life. You see the busyness is also impeding and delaying the healing. Despite the busyness, the problems persist.

The remedy is to "be still."

The healing comes from acknowledgment and process of what has happened in that context of painful events. Instead what has happened continues to 'haunt" them and shape their lives until they are able to process with a professional their trauma.

However, everyone does not necessarily experience a trauma, but they stay busy for other reasons.

As you read further, I will discuss how busyness could be destructive to healing.

This is what I learned from busyness in my own life. It has some advantages, but also some disadvantages, including delayed healing. This is my story. I shared parts of with you earlier, so I will be brief and try not repeat myself.

After my divorce, I sought a means to feel better, and unconsciously that was through staying busy. But it did not start out this way. It started as having to survive the disappointment of being divorced, along with raising a young child.

While going through that change, I was trying to find a safe, affordable place to stay, while continuing to work and stay in school. I asked myself, "How do I do this, being a working single parent?" It was scary, because I had defined myself by my marriage, being attached to someone else. I did not know who I was, and actually this was an opportunity for me to get to know who I was. But instead I became busy and bitter toward God.

Though not admittedly, I just could not understand why my marriage did not work out and why was I going through this, especially, since "I had done everything right" according to what I thought the societal and traditional religious standards were at that time.

So in my self-righteous mind, I thought, "I graduated from high school and undergraduate college, married my college 'sweetheart', moved to a big city, pursued graduate studies at an Ivy League...so why, God, did You not keep your end of the bargain?"

Wow, the arrogance of self-righteousness.

But what I did not understand was that I had free will and I made the choice to get married in my youth and ignorance.

God did not choose this plan. This was my plan and I wanted to God to follow my own "instructions."

I was too busy to listen to what God wanted for my life.

I regressed to explain the mindset that was in, the best possible scenario. We had no idea what stood before us or how things would turn out.

I knew God, but not the way I KNOW HIM today. I only knew of Him in the religious sense, but not in the spiritual sense. I knew to go to church on Sundays and Wednesday night Bible class and to pray every night. But how about all the time in between—daily living, mindset, prayer, meditation, fasting, and having conversations with God?

Although I had conversations with God regularly as child, because this was a natural inclination for me do so; I had become so distracted that I stopped being still long enough to feel God's presence and hear His voice.

Coming back to the subject of "busyness", what started out as necessity became a way of living. Busyness was a way for me to place myself in control and plan everything within my own power.

All the time God was blessing me and showing me favor. Not because I was doing everything right, but it was because of HIS love and grace.

God never left me, but was longing for me to reach out and call on him, praise Him in good and bad times, to acknowledge that all good things were coming from Him.

I failed to fully heal during my years as single woman. I was in the process of becoming. I now realized that my experiences have made me perfect for my purpose.

BUSYNESS leads us away to distract us from what is truly there. It is just another tool, an evil tool that hides us from our healing, our purpose. It one of the many tools we use like sex, alcohol, drugs, physical sickness, or food to keep us from our true selves, our authenticity, or our destiny. Most of all our busyness prevents us healing from that pain.

If we never stop to acknowledge that pain, we are not just hurting ourselves, but the others around us. But most importantly, are we really loving ourselves when we work beyond exhaustion and never ever rest? How are we truly experiencing God's love?

How are we allowing God to truly do his work in our lives when are constantly busy?

We are acknowledging God's grace, his wonderful grace to allow to us rest peacefully in his presence and give all our pain and sorrow to him.

"Come to me, all of you who are weary and burdened, and I will give you rest." (Matthew 11:28, NKJV)

I did not take time to rest, be silent and listen to God. Instead of being still, I was staying busy and trying to do everything in my own power. I should have silenced my inner self and moved out of the way and allowed God to lead the way and do my healing.

It is important that you are silent and still, so that you can acknowledge pain and fear, then face it and release it to the Lord!!

Self-Pity

What is self-pity? Self-pity is feeling sorry for yourself when feel you have lost and fought in vain. In self-pity, you are thinking about the thing that happened to you, like how terrible you are. But we sometimes forget about the greater picture, which is that there is not a reason to feel sorry for yourself when focus on the love of God.

When I felt self-pity, I would read Psalm 73. It actually talks about people who are doing wrong and it feels like doing right is all in vain. However, in this passage it also talks about how it appears that the wicked are getting away with their wickedness.

At the end of the chapter it shows that the righteous prevail. It explains God is always faithful and victorious. And since you are with God, you are victorious too. Therefore your righteousness is not in vain.

"Truly God is good to Israel, to such as are pure in heart. But as for me, my feet had almost stumbled; my steps had nearly slipped. For I was envious of the boastful when I saw the prosperity of the wicked. For there are no pangs in their death, but their strength is firm. They are not in trouble as other men, nor are they plagued like other men. Therefore pride serves as their necklace; violence covers them like a garment. Their eyes bulge with abundance; they have more than heart could wish. They scoff and speak wickedly concerning oppression; they speak loftily. They set their mouth against the heavens, and their tongue walks through the earth. Therefore his people return here, and waters of a full cup are drained by them. And they say, "How does God know? And is there knowledge in the Most High?" Behold, these are the ungodly, who are always at ease; they increase in riches. Surely I have cleansed my heart in vain, and washed my hands in innocence. For all day long I have been plagued, and chastened every morning. If I had said, "I will speak thus," behold, I would have been untrue to the generation of Your children. When I thought how to understand this, it was too painful for me until I went into the sanctuary of God; then I understood their end." Psalms 73:1-17 (NKJV)

Also in another passage, it deals with strife and staying in peace when you feel like you're getting the 'short end of the stick' or staying in peace and avoiding strife. In the story, in Genesis 13, it initially appears that a Lot had gotten much more than Abraham, but at the end it was not so. Abram did not argue with his Lot over the land, but stayed in peace and let him (his relative) choose first. See Genesis 13: 14-15 (KJV).

"**14 And the Lord said unto Abram, after Lot was separated from him, lift up now thine eyes, and look from the place where art northward, and southward, and eastward, and westward: 15For all the land which thou seest, to thee I will give it, and to thy seed forever.**"

This is an illustration of how God works and how peace works and how things work out for a good will we do it God's way. Therefore we should be careful what we say and what we do, and understand that God is in control and God sees all and knows all. Also, this demonstrates that God keeps his promises and where there is no vision, there is no progress. God provided a vision for Abram to see what was promised to him in above quote. In our busyness, we must learn to become still (mentally at peace) and allow God to work to continue in our lives.

Silence

What is Silence? I believe it is the act of being quiet; it is the act of not being seen, being invisible. Silence is not just referring to lack of sound, but it also refers to lack of presence. When an individual verbal communication is silenced, this is unfortunate, but when an individual silences her thoughts and emotions, this is a tragedy. Sometimes life circumstances silences our voices and trauma, and many is the culprit of our silencing of our voices.

Charity's Story

During her early childhood, her mother became a single mother raising her and her sister, after divorce. She was so close to her mom. She was quite attached and loved her more than anyone in the world. She looked up to her mother, feeling that her mother was greatest and could do no wrong indeed. She explained that her closeness with her mother may have perhaps been a result of her distance from her father. Many memories do not carry with her before the age 5. She explains, "What I carry is my emotion when I return to those environments, and people, I become silent once again. To me silence was a way of survival and a way of protecting myself, by gaining information and by staying unharmed or rejected."

But over years, she felt that she had no voice, and that she felt that she was just a bystander and observer to all that was occurring. She could only listen in silence. This is how she lived her life, in silence, staying in the background as instructed. This became the nature of her relationships with her ex-husbands, her friends, and her career. She had learned how to love others in the mist of silence, learning to negate herself and who she was in order to make others feel more comfortable. She did not realize that her protection comes from God, and that she did not have to work so hard at protecting herself. For efforts to do so, resulted in failure; because she trusted herself and not God.

Reflections

What are some childhood memories that impacted you?
What are some childhood memories that kept you from
healing? How is un-forgiveness of your childhood events
hindering your growth, your blessing, and ultimately, your
healing? Do you feel that God is protecting you? Write down
all the ways that God has protected you over the years.

_____

_____

_____

_____

_____

Charity's Story

Parts of Charity's Story, are not her own, but are told to her by others in which she has created as her own reality and understanding. This is her earliest accounts of when, what, how she began learning about herself even when she did not know it.

She explained, "In those times, when I was growing up I was often misunderstood, and since my voice was silenced, there was little room for explanation. I learned not fight or express my needs or desires. I was simply a blank slate on the wall to be of service to others because my voice was not relevant, or so I thought."

She explained that this thinking may have come about in her when she would have periods of expression. But at those few times, it seemed that there was punitive results which discouraged her from attempting that again. She thought that the conflict was too much to deal with and it was NOT a normal part of life's process. This is not true."

She explained, "Conflict that occurs in life teaches us about ourselves and others. This was a place of learning which she had missed out on; this would play out in my relationships, including personal, business, and work relationships."

She had learned not to fight. She had learned flight, shown by becoming passive, invisible and irrelevant.

The woman talked about her experience of silence. As a result of her silence she was kept in the background and overlooked. Silencing her voice became second nature and was no longer forced. Granted, there is a time and place for silence, for one to hold her tongue, but to do it all the time is quite extreme. Silencing yourself can come from trauma, rejection, and quite simply, a learned behavior.

In her case, one would describe her as an extremely timid, quiet child whose silence continued throughout college in certain settings. She explained that her silence was most profound and noticeable by her friends who knew her outside of her home when they visited her as an adult in the presence of her home of origin.

They told her that it appeared as if she would go into a hiding place, a shell of silence when in that dynamic and they said it was a striking difference in how she was outside the home. It was a dichotomous persona that was like night and day for those who knew well.

In settings outside the home, she was confident, fun, witty, smart, social, and opinionated. However, her presentation in the home was of a stark difference. This presentation of her persona carried into her relationships with men. When she became part of an intimate relationship, all too often she became the passive, submissive servant with no opinions and no demand. As a result, she attracted domineering, insecure men who felt more "manly" when coupled with someone who was passive.

These were messages that were coming toward her, reinforced by her beliefs gathered from her religious worship and home. Now, she did not believe that this was the way that was it purposely done. Charity explained, "When I witnessed domestic violence as a child, my mind had no way of interpreting it or understanding such violence and conflict, therefore, I retreated to place of silence and peace. I then discovered God and began to talk my Creator on daily basis. As a child, this is how my many hours of playtime were spent in my own little world; just me and God alone."

She further stated, "You know how some children have imaginary friends? This was my place of solitude, speaking with God."

Charity understood early on that he would be her Father, since no physical father existed in her household. As time had it, she would cling to her mother who was her "hero" in her mind. When she also had an additional protector, her sister from the outsiders who misunderstood her as weak and wanted to challenge her by exploiting or abusing her. She thought that she was shielded from all this by two people who encountered multiple traumas in their own lives.

The danger of silence is that it causes the offence to perpetuate. Silencing the voice makes not only individuals passive, but also numbs them to life. They go through life without experiencing all God-given emotions. In this case, for her, silence becomes a living death.

Trials and Tribulations

I remember hearing older people talking about staying at peace when going through trials and tribulations, but I did not understand it at first. "Stay at peace" when someone treats you wrong; don't become bitter. I would hear, "God will repay you for all that has been done wrong to you," and was reminded that:

"The Lord said unto my Lord, Sit thou at my right hand, until I make thine enemies thy footstool." Psalms 110:1 (KJV)

This is repeated also in Hebrews 10:13 (KJV), "From henceforth expecting till his enemies be made his footstool."

And again in Matthew 22:44 (KJV), "The Lord said unto my Lord, Sit thou on my right hand, till I make thine enemies thy footstool?"

Throughout the Bible, it give us instruction on how to deal with life's problems and situations. As you study, you will hear and understand the simplicity of the word and message as it become real and clear to you. This is where peace comes in, understanding that God is the Protector and Provider of all things. When we understand this, life becomes more peaceful, and we are able to overcome many things, because we understand that God is fighting all our battles and that we are never alone. We should not attempt to function in our own strength, but in the strength of our Creator. It is with knowledge that I pursued that passions and dreams with talents which I am blessed. It is in the times of tribulation and lack when we grow the most and learn the most. We should not rush the process, experience the pain, the tearfulness, the hurt, the disappointment and know that God has a greater plan.

Because the trials and tribulations are less about the situation and is less about the other person, and more about you, we must be patient as things unfold. Once we understand that this is a process toward our greatness, toward our development, then we take it as it comes. We praise the Lord in our building in our process toward fulfilling life's destiny chosen by God.

All in all, simply put, I wanted things to fall into my hands, without God, without grace. I know that's what I wanted. I wanted something miraculous happen without learning and growing and working. I wanted God to follow the order of my instructions and my request. I did not know that this was backwards.

But faith without works is dead. And most would say things can't fall in your hands.

Why does this happen to some and not to others? We only know what we've witnessed, but not behind the scenes.

You see, sometimes those prayers do not come into fruition because you are still being developed to be able to receive those gifts. Or maybe or you have received the gifts, but were not thankful enough to acknowledge those gifts.

All experiences are molding for what is at hand right know, making our imperfections have a purpose, making us perfect for the task we were assigned to in this life. For without these experiences, we are likely the right person for the job! I finally began to realize that I no longer regret my experiences because I am perfect for the job that has been placed before me.

Or simply because we don't ask big, but we ask small, not believing what we say. God is all powerful and owner and creator or all things.

What is it that we truly believe? Do really believe in what we speak? Or maybe we pray for what we want, and not for God's will. Jesus lived and died for us. Should we then live for the one who has died for us? For it is written, "And that he died for all, that they should not live for themselves, but unto him which died for them, and rose again." – 2 Corinthians 5:15 (AMP)

Emotional Pain

"Fear not, for I am with you; be not dismayed, for I am your God. I will strengthen, yes, I will help you, I will uphold you with My righteous right hand." **Isaiah 41:10 (NKJV)**

Charity's Story

She was a woman, but on the inside she felt like child. She was searching for something new within herself, which was very different, because she was accustomed to looking on outside of herself for answer. However, from a year of trauma, multiple tragedies, and change, she learned some things the hard way–by going through them.

She learned to trust the voice within herself that was trying to move her forward and protect her many times. The pain and disappointment was not all in vain–but it was for a purpose which God only knows. She knew that she must now listen to the inner voice, the inner spirit to guide her path to her heart's desire to what she needs more than what she wants.

The Spirit knows this, but her intellect was clueless. Her mind has been focused on her own desires and not the will of the Spirits and what feeds the Spirit. This path is only the one that God can lead her on, and she says, "Help me, God, help me, help me in my ignorance. Help me on the path to reveal my revelation and give me the motivation and courage to do so."

What she did not yet understand, is that she was still in shock of all of what had come to pass and was trying to find a way to put it all back together without dying emotionally. She yelled in her spirit, "Lord, help me.....I need your help!"

And the tears of mourning and loss began to flow, but can't quite come out because the wound was so deep and she says, "Lord, it hurts so.... It's too painful to cry or to speak of what has come to pass."

Trauma comes in various forms with many layers, with one life changing event on top of another event. What is one to do? How was she to survive it all? How was she to make it without dying on the inside, falling into a deep depression? But at last, she felt that parts of her was already dying and while she was steady covering her pain, GOD was steady revealing and protecting her in the mist of the fire.

So some would ask, "What is this *trauma*?" and say, "People die every day, people divorce every day, people have miscarriages every day, people have people used others for money every day, people are deceived daily. What makes your situation extraordinary?"

But does this happen all at one time to everybody? Does what everybody thinks even matter in a situation when a person who is going through the pain? She would not allow herself to grieve because, like I said, her pain was much too great to cry. And she heard this: "I'm here and I have always been with you."

She was mourning a great loss of time, of life, of confidence. For David well demonstrated that (Psalms 56:1-4, **NKJV**):

"Be merciful to me, O God, for man would swallow me up; Fighting all the day he oppresses me. My enemies would hound me all day, For there are many who fight against me, O Most High. Whenever I am afraid, I will trust in You. In God (I will praise his word), In God I have put my trust; I will not fear. What can flesh do to me?"

Mourning

"The righteous cry, and the Lord heareth, and delivereth them out of their troubles." Psalms 34:17 (KJV)

How does one mourn when the wound is so fresh? What does one do? How does one see fit to express when trying to be strong in the pain? Are we avoiding vulnerability in order to avoid the pain?

Why is it so important to get immediately past it? Don't we need to feel the pain? Is there a need to find some understanding in ourselves to feel it, so that it can be revealed, so that we can heal? How is ignoring and avoiding the pain going to allow us to get better? How is it going to allow us to be receptive to new love if we only learn from pain to be numb and uncaring? We do not truly learn how to forgive if we decide to avoid or ignore it.

When the pain is so fresh, how are we to just ignore it all as if it never happened, going into that superwoman mode until we wake and realize that we were not truly living? We were just existing and walking through life. Truly God wants more of us. He does not want us to exist this way. What I have learned that helps me is that I needed to feel and acknowledge the pain. I needed to feel all the emotions associated with an event, trauma, or crisis. I needed to feel again, instead of being numb and emotionless. I needed to feel all my emotions, happiness, sadness, anger instead of covering it with emotionless nonchalant mask I needed to cry and scream to the top of my lungs to what has hurt me so that the pain will not persist inside and slowly kill all feeling, killing my zest for life. I am saying this because I have allowed it to happen. This usually appears as depression, anger, anxiety, or irritability because the real issue has not been dealt with. I now understood that healing began with feeling everything, no matter how hard or painful.

Reflections

Have you ever been hurt so bad that it was too painful to cry? Have you ever felt judged by others in your pain? How did you deal with it? Are you still dealing with it? How should you process your pain and move through it?

_____

_____

_____

_____

_____

_____

Your pain is your pain, your truth is your truth. What you know to be true does not need validation from other people. This is the power of your instinct (intuition, spirit, God's voice). This is your power. When this is acknowledged, you have given yourself the power back and permission to heal and move forward.

Sometimes it feels as if the pain is just too much to bear. You don't know what to do, but just sing, pray, and cry, and sometimes it's just too hard to cry. At times you can't sleep or eat, you can only do what God has called you do. One thing I do know is this: Healing takes a long time if you don't know where to start or how to start. I say let's start from the beginning.

Destiny, Healing, & Fear.

Destiny is what we were purposed to do, sent here to do, but yet we have many distractions as we go. Destiny is what God has purposed us to do, to become, or to fulfill. As we become closer to path of destiny, there are enemies (distractions), which become more aggressive in preventing us from achieving it. Have you ever found yourself thinking, "That this is what I am supposed to do!" and your soul leaps? But then sickness, financial challenges, the family commitments, the discouragement, the negative self-thoughts, the feelings of inadequacy, the children, the job, the boss, the tiredness, friends, boyfriends are some of ways the enemy uses to prevent you from reaching your destiny. There are lessons which I have learned during my healing journey.

The belief that things will be easy in this life is a fallacy. But those things, as I have learned, are sometimes things which are made for us to develop the position in our destiny. We are faced with these "small" challenges so that we can learn how deal with bigger challenges in the future. With that in mind, God makes no mistakes.

The second thing which I have learned is **"Trust the Lord in Everything,"** to consult with the Lord in all things and in all things consult with the Lord. This is a something that I did not realize in much of my adult life. I had heard people say this repeatedly, heard this said in church, read it in the Bible, but it was not down within my spirit.

In my mind, I felt that I had to control everything so I would be safe, secure. I was the master, or so I thought, planning out my life's next step. When things did not work out, I was greatly disappointed and blamed God instead of finding my refuge in God.

I blamed God for failure in my first marriage, I felt that he had left me all alone. And this was not plan. My plan was to get married have 4 children, stay at home for a while, work some, and be married for a lifetime. That was my plan but I did not follow God's blueprint for my life.

I had a plan for my life and I wanted God to follow it!

However, God's blueprint is for me to trust in Him in all things, to put Him first. However, I learned that God's love is not a condemning love, for it is a forgiving love that will chase you down.

Oh, how this is a wonderful gift to acknowledge. I say acknowledge because the gift has always been there. God gave his **only** son so that we could have life and be freed from our sins. God chases us down passionately even when we are in our sins, and all the more, because he loves us. Remember this: GOD's love is not a condemning love, but it's a forgiving love. Once we understand this, we can live fearlessly.

Thirdly, this is what I have learned about fear. Fear is a means to block you from your destiny, keeping you from opening the door that God has already given us access to. We just have to trust in him and walk through that door.

Fear is something that I have misunderstood for some time. There a difference between fear and discernment and it's dangerous to get the two confused.

In my life, I have gotten what I thought was fear to get me to go in the wrong direction, but in reality what I was experiencing was not fear, but was discernment. It was discernment that told me not marry, it was discernment that told me not invest my savings in a business, it was discernment which told me the state and nature of my relationships, but I did not listen. I did not listen because I thought it was fear *speaking*.

Once I began to listen to God clearly, I gained courage to move on what discernment was telling me and could not be deceived into believing that it was only fear. God has blessed me with this gift and I must acknowledge and ask Him when I am unsure. This is what I have learned.

Healing and Fear

Can one heal, if there is fear? This a question that wherein the answer has been provided. The answer is absolutely not!

Individuals who suffer with Post Traumatic Stress Disorder (PTSD, APA, 2013) cannot heal because of persistent and generalized fear. The fear is difficult to overcome because of the persistent avoidance of what is feared, the feeling associated with event, the guilt associated with the event, the shame associated with the event.

Once individuals can face their fear in PTSD then they are on their way to recovery, on their way to healing. Many of the therapies for PTSD deal with confronting the trauma, the thing that caused the fear, in order to begin the healing process.

Those individuals who have suffered a significant loss have fears about the next step, fears that "it" will happen again, have fears that they are not adequate. These are all lies that our mind tells us self once a trauma has occurred.

It Doesn't Bother Me Anymore

"It doesn't bother you when you talk truthfully about your past; there is no more shame and no more guilt. You know God's power is Healing!" – Alex Young

While talking to a girlfriend about the dating experiences after my divorce, I was grounded to find that I felt no longer ashamed and no longer hurt by all the disappointments of past relationships. I had maneuvered my way through dating without a clue of the "game" and without listening to GOD. I thought I knew exactly what I was doing until I got caught up in my continuous repetition of encountering the same mistakes over and over again. This continued until I finally realized learned what I needed to learn about myself and love. Love is God and God is Love. What I did not understand was love, in its fullest essence, because I had not learned how to fully love myself with all my flaws and inconsistences.

I was hard on myself and those that came into my life. My perfect was a mode that they could not fit, because it was one that I could not fit. So they just went with the flow, perhaps, they felt that they could not get any more that split moment they had with me, when all the time I was wishing for more consistency while I was providing them with more inconsistencies. My inconsistencies where revealed in my actions.

It was all because I myself did not know who I was or what I wanted. Actually, I knew what I wanted, but did not believe that I could get it, I did not believe that God could bless me in that way. It was something I could not imagine, having a loving relationship with God as the head to the individuals involved.

I did not know me, because I was trying to fit a mode that was not me. It was for someone else. The "me" of who I was waiting to be discovered, and God was patiently waiting to show me. All I had to do is to simply ask, open the door, and be still and listen for a minute. With all the disappointment and sadness along with the continuous feelings of loneliness, it was not a man that I needed, but it was God. It was only God that I needed to trust through all this.

It was and is by his grace that I continue to live bountifully without shame, full of forgiveness, love, and empathy for others. It was only my Father who delivered from the shame of dating mistakes, realities, learning, foolishness, feeling tricked, lost, and unloved, feeling that I was the victim.

Did I provide others with a superficial experience of who I was by shading it with sex, not giving them the opportunity to know who I was? Possibly not caring who they fully were, in order to avoid hurt? But alas, hurt comes anyway, because the truth has no way of hiding, even when we try to cover it with lies. EVEN WHEN

WE TRY TO COVER IT WITH LIES. Let me say that again—even when we try to cover it with lies.

In a conversation with a friend, we were discussing the naiveté of choices made as younger selves. During this conversation about dating experiences, I realized how naïve I was in my choices. I no longer felt ashamed of my past. Those people may have reflected some part of myself, whether it was the father figure that I unknowingly desired, a friend, or family—it all came down to my internal self and what I was ignoring.

Maybe I just was not ready to hear what God was trying to teach, trying show me, and alas— through this series of traumas, death of three miscarriages, verbal, physical, and sexual abuse from my second marriage, I finally heard God. I was beginning to understand the grace of God and all His power.

And I said this prayer, "I thank You, Dear Lord, for your grace and power and all the love you have given to me, even when I did not feel that I deserve it. I thank you, O Lord, for your wonderful, wonderful, grace. Grace, what a wonderful thing for us imperfect people. There is no shame in perfect love. All is forgiven, all in love. I thank you, Dear Lord!"

Transparency

The scary thing about transparency is that you may learn something about yourself that you thought others did not already know. You are afraid that others will see before you see it, and will judge you harshly in the way in which you would have judge someone who was in your same shoes.

Is it the fear of transparency about you or the other people? The more you understand that other people's perceptions of you are only a reflection of what you see yourself as, then the more you will understand that it's not about you, it's about them and what they are feeling about themselves. Transparency, what about it? Is it something to fear or something to embrace? Let us ponder on this. Well, I have pondered over it, and healed people would tell you to embrace it. What factor makes you embrace it? The healing power of God, the grace of God can give us the strength to face our biggest fears and challenges. For me it was being transparent. Because with transparency comes trust. Trust in God to allow you discern when to be transparent.

The way of trying, the way of doing, is to understand the gifts which God has given to us. We are spiritual when we don't acknowledge or recognize it. It is then and there, where we begin to disconnect from the very essence of who we are. It is then that we must work toward and into our gifts to discover and truly understand our humanity. What makes us human, is the part that we began to understand about ourselves, the things we accept and the things we don't, and the reasons for these beliefs. Through this process of analysis, it is important that we continue to work toward the progress through our flaws to love which not seen in mirror. With this understanding and realization comes healing, forgiveness of self and others.

Only when we are STILL, and ACKNOWLEDGE God, is when we began to experience our greatness, understand who we truly are, and have the courage to go forward with what is already within us. Many times our feeling of inadequacy creeps in and we feel like we cannot or should not be doing it.

The more that I think about this, the Spirit tells me to persist in my gift to share with others. My desires which I have spoken to God on occasions, actually often, when I discover them, I know that God already knows. They are what YOU already know and have for me to rediscover and follow through on. God was able to turn my pain into something beautiful, to help and serve others, but most of all to help me heal and forgive myself so that I may leave my past behind.

Some of the greatest people have come out of the most pain and unfortunate circumstances. Just look at the lineage of Jesus Christ. Everyone in his was bloodline was not perfect and without stain. Just then, the plan is not to have perfect people, but understand GOD's power and transformation. For we have only to challenge ourselves, for the enemy is outside ourselves.

Thoughts of feeling that, "I am not enough" or "I can NOT do this" or "Who am I kidding, this is not art, this is nothing" are lies. Or to hear others say to you minimize your creativity or don't really care when you share with them good news of successes after going through your trials. You began to learn to be quiet about your successes and thank God for this discernment and advisement and the blessings. You have to ask for discernment on these things.

I am always listening. For example, I was having a conversation with colleague and he was telling me about how people can sometimes shoot an idea down before you even get started. He was talking about how many people forsake trying something new due to feeling inadequate and never pursue their dream because they are stopping themselves based on lack of support. And as he was speaking, I was thinking how many times I started on my path to my destiny, to my dream and it was shot down—only to have me end up frustrated, discouraged and unfulfilled. What have I forsaken when an idea of mine was discouraged, or shot down by family or a friend?

This colleague went on to talk about how this types of people don't often proceed because they feel they don't have any support. But many times you must proceed with caution without support and proceed in faith, understanding you don't always need others to proceed with your dream or ideas. You proceed because this is what God gave you to do, therefore you have no choice. This is no longer about you! **You must not compete with God, but rather allow Him to complete the good work that is in you.**

Getting to a Better Place

When we don't know the direction we are going in and it does not seem better, only appears worse. The road becomes weary and we began to wonder when we will we get to a better place. Then tragedy strikes and we go a dark place and we perceive it as the end, but it is not the end. We later learn that our ending is our beginning and we had to relearn out destiny.

Recently, the man that raised me, my stepfather (I will affectionately call him my father) had a seemingly mild stroke, so we thought. We thought that he would be returning home shortly after 2.5 weeks of therapy, but as time progressed, he became less responsive and more ill. He refused to eat and he became worse rather than better. The doctors said that he only had a few weeks to live and suggested hospice. As he lay there in the hospital there was such an outpouring of support from family and friends–but there was no comfort for my mother's sorrow. We pray and cry out to God, but do we really believe in the possibility of his miracle?

My father was tired and was ready to leave; our prayers may not have been the same as his. Only God know this. This is a place ing for healing and our family continued to understand the love and grace of God in the midst of death.

This is my prayer: God, tell us what to do, how to get to a better place in understanding–teach us, oh Dear Lord.

Grieving, Loss, & Memory

How can we heal from those we have lost? It is as if part of ourselves has died, because life seems dull after their departure and time is seen a valued commodity that we once took for granted. Is it possible to fully heal? What does it take to heal?

It takes acceptance of what the wound is, what the loss is, being patient, and giving yourself time to feel all those emotions. Healing requires you to laugh, to cry, to be angry, to be frustrated, to experience the loneliness, missing the one who has gone. It's missing the convenience of picking up the telephone and saying, "Hello, Dad, I was just calling to check on you," and to hear his voice saying, "Hey, baby girl."

Grieving takes on another meaning. Meaning that grieving is not just loss but is acceptance of your pain, remembrance of the one is no longer with us, and period to reflect on the time we have left in this life. However, time is the gift that God has provided to us.

Time Is a Gift

What is it that God wants us to hear and to see? How God does want us to love, be happy, and be joyful? This life is full of mystery, full of the unknowns, but what is known is only here. Only now do we have this moment in time to live, to fulfill our purpose.

How many chances do we get before time overtakes us? I finally understand what's most valuable: my time, not my money.

For the saying is, "Time is money and money is time," but most importantly we were tricked into believing that money is the most important. With only time can we build, create, and we can heal and learn. With time, we love and learn to love more freely. With time destruction is dissolved and joy can manifest.

Time, oh, our precious time. It is all that we have, right here, right now. In time is when the sick can become well and again, and see a new life. Oh, precious Time, we love thee, for time has been ignored for far too long. For with God, our Creator has provided us with time and with that time, there is GRACE. Grace to make a better life, to create a new beginning. Think about it, how are you spending your time, this precious gift we have been given on THIS day? What are we to do with it? We were given free will to do with it what we will.

COMING THROUGH THE PAIN

"To console those who mourn in Zion, to give them beauty for ashes, the oil of joy for mourning, the garment of praise for the spirit of heaviness; that they may be called trees of righteousness, the planting of the Lord that he may be glorified." Isaiah 61:3 (NKJV)

Missing Your Purpose

Many times we live our lives and our days with a multitude of "to dos". In our busyness, we seem to always fall short of something. We may fall short of time, energy, and at times the task itself. We are scattered here and there by our chores and the responsibilities of others. It is here where we may become entangled in this routine of a multitude of tasks, missing the very point of it all. That's right, the point of it all, and the point of your life, or let's say the purpose of your life.

I ask myself, am I doing things to fulfill my purpose? Do I know my purpose? Do you know that you have a purpose? Have you missed the clues that were presented to show you essentially who you are in your busyness? When we understand what's important, we pay less attention to what's not. This what is meant in part by living on purpose—to live and not simply exist, to live out your destiny, your purpose! Are you being still enough to recognize what is purposed for your life? Are you paying attention?

Paying Attention

"When living in this life, there are intentions for our lives, however, when we faced with our adversary as we draw near to destiny, it at these crossroads where we face it fearlessly or are overcome by it. It is then when we learn who we are. It is here where we learn what our shortcomings are and what strengths are. Either way, if we pay attention, we learn, we conquer, and overcome when we pay attention." -Young 4/20/2017

What is at the forefront of our minds is our intention, and our intention is what guides our day and our moments. It is here that we find who we truly are, if we pay attention.

Things aren't always what they seem to be and what they should be. Our lives go forward and toward a will and a way, despite our best plans.

When things don't turn out that way, we feel as if we have failed and that we are less than what we really are. This is most unfortunate, since at times our best plans are not our true calling and not our true destiny. We often miss our true calling because we are listening to people outside ourselves. We are not quieting ourselves enough to even just pay attention to ourselves, to that inner voice. Some call it many things, like intuition or instinct. In its true essence, the calling from within—which is for your highest good—is God informing us of who we were born to become, and an ending that He saw for us before the beginning.

Each person was born for a purpose and reason. The dreams of who we can become and our highest potential is attainable. The theme for the past few weeks of my life has been "PAYING ATTENTION." I should be paying attention. Otherwise, I will miss some important information, perhaps, something that could be life-changing and provide some peaceful perspective in the here and now of this day. Many time we miss the point of the moment because we are pivoting into our future plans, or reflecting on our past when it is now that we should be attending to. The now, the present is what we should be living in. Not in the past of what I should have or could have done, but simply living in the present.

Right now, is it God who trying to get your attention? He is always present. But we are not paying attention to our gifts which confront us in the now of our lives. Much of our time is wasted in planning our own future and in our past. We are focused in those two time phases but miss our current being, our "currency" of our life of how we are spending our time.

We are missing our gifts because the focus is on something other than the now. I had to acknowledge that all I have is right now. All you have is right now...yes, all we have is right now.

Maybe, just maybe, if we could live our lives in this way, the pain would fade faster and the healing will pursue us instead of us pursuing it.

It is through my life circumstance, my pain, my loss, that I needed to heal and it is through this evolution that it occurred to me, that I should be paying attention. That I should be paying attention to what is before me, paying attention to what's keeping me from my work, my gift, and the creativity that I been blessed with.

So I ask myself, Is it me that is acting or serving as the distraction or is it others? Maybe it's a combination thereof.

Don't distracted by your past, use it! Use your past and trials as a means to heal and prepare you for what comes next!

The Job Phenomenon (in Bible, Job, KJV): When everything goes wrong in your life, and everyone is blaming you for it, saying you must have done something wrong. Don't get caught into believing the lie that you always cause your trials and tribulations. In some things we are powerless, but we are not powerless in our response to it.

We are powerful in in our response if we remain steadfast, listen the inner spirit, ask for the guidance of the Holy Spirit, and pay attention to what is really happening. Maybe there is no logical reason for its occurrence, maybe it only that occurrence something of the spiritual nature that is meant to prove you, examine the heart of you, the inner self as a man or woman, or to examine the spirit. To examine the truth of your being and very nature of who you are as a person.

Under the fire, truth reveals itself, the good or the bad. Where there is no fire, how can you be sure of the heart?

When all is lovely and wonderful in life, with no stress, would we ever have the cure to illnesses, great musical compositions, human rights movements, poets, passionate singers, engineers, and multiplicity of talents and gifts revealed? Would we ever know if any such thing exists? Perhaps, we would never know if we let the "Job Phenomenon" overtakes us, making us believe that is something wrong with us, that "it must be something you have done wrong, otherwise this would not be happening to you," or it is something that you are doing to cause this catastrophic events. You need to go to the doctor. There are cases when we unconsciously or consciously engage in self-destructive behaviors that leads us from our destiny, but I am by no means talking about these events in referencing the Job Phenomenon. I am talking about events which may occur without one's power and engagement in the process. As the cliché is said, "Bad things happen to good people all the time."

But many of us do not believe this cliché and are usually skeptical about the events and judge the suffering person as the cause; thereby becoming less supportive and more destructive to their healing and recovery, if they were to listen and empathize with faulty beliefs.

At times, beliefs are likely faulty because of limited experiences, allowing others to pass judgment and to be an "expert" in their circumstances.

So the question is, how does one know the difference between a trial and something they have brought on themselves? The answer can be complicated if we are not truthful, or rather, if we do not know how to be truthful to ourselves. This is a whole other chapter though.

Many times, when are going in a certain directions, something speaks to us and tells us the answers to many of our questions if we just pay attention. Here it is again, pay attention. Do we need to get the answers from our friends, family, neighbors, or our preacher? Probably not—always, many times the answer is there and most times, we just don't know how to pay attention.

This is my prayer, "Please, God, allow me to pay attention to what you are telling me, to what you are showing me while seeking you in all my questions and listen to answers, while being courageous enough to obey your answers. In your loving name I pray. I thank you, Dear Lord, for it has already been done. Thank you."

Still Moving, But it Does not Feel like It

What happens you are making progress, but you do not feel like you are? It seems like you are standing still and all you can see is the same in whatever you trying to work on, to improve, create, or expand on. What that happens, when it feels like you are at stand still, although you continue to put in the energy and time, it this a time to give up and quit? Or is it simply an illusion that nothing is happening, when everyone around you may see changes but you don't recognize those changes because of your deep involvement in the process of change?

It seems that stuff just don't bother you anymore. That's when you know that you have allowed you creator to work on you and stopped striving to become who are able to be. At these times, motivation seems to decrease and distractions come in to play, from energy busters, endless chores, new projects, and family concerns, and of course exercise, eating right, making deadlines.

Okay, you get the point. There are endless lists of distractions to keep us from our God-given assignment, whatever that may be to you. It is your responsibility to fulfill it, discipline yourself to stay the course.

That's what has happened to me over the past week while I have not worked on this manuscript. There was distraction after distraction to propel from its continuation and ultimately its completion. The depth of the distraction and discouragement tells me the importance of completing it, that I must complete it. It is my responsibility to do so.

The fact that I am sitting here now working on it, shows the progress of healing that God has allowed me to have in these past few months. How I started off was quite different than where it is now. It has not ended for me. Healing is in motion, in progress constantly, for those who are closest to me, for this has been my prayer and my intention. With this prayer and intention, there are revelations of pulling back of many layers of the wound in which the process is too difficult for those involved, including myself. How do I react to others?

How do you react to others healing, when their WOUNDS ARE SO DEEP, and they do not even know where to start or how to heal? What is your reaction and you action in facilitating this? Is this your responsibility to facilitate this, I ask, is it my responsibility to do this within my family? Here is my answer. I do nothing.

I react in different ways than usual which often leads to opposition and anger by the wounded parties, because they feel abandoned. This feeling stems from co-dependency, where the other person repeatedly sacrifices who he or she is for the sake of the KEEPING THE PEACE in the relationship that has no peace. It has no peace because there is no peace in the individual, because this is what is perpetuating the growing the wound and the continued illness.

We are taught to KEEP the PEACE instead of MAKING THE PEACE.

So I need to stop and define what peace is in its most literal sense. According to the definition, peace is "freedom from disturbance, quiet and tranquility." Let me emphasize this because I am amazed at the power of simple meaning of peace. Here it is: "Freedom from DISTURBANCE, Quiet and Tranquility."

So, in essence, a person in pain and who is wounded had no peace. Therefore, it makes sense that others who are around that person would have no peace. There is likely to be an adverse reaction toward those who have peace. Because this "peace" is a foreign entity to the wounded individual, in the midst of pain.

So you ask, what is my reaction, what is it that you would have me do in the midst of this pain that other people are experiencing?

This is what I did. I silenced myself, shut myself up, and gave it to God. I sought to answer through prayer and gave to God.

It is my understanding that it is only God who has the power to heal and renew. All power flows from the Lord. God is love, and through that healing—physical, emotional, and psychological healing—I understand that my role is authentic rather than good.

Although, in society we are taught to be more "good" than authentic, when being good and not really living in truth and does not lead to healing and growth, but rather it stumps you, shrouded in traditions and etiquette, rather than authenticity and love.

The questions we always ask about love is how do I know he/she loves me? How do I show love? How is love expressed?

The problem is that we don't truly understand what love is. We see love as noun or an adjective rather than word that denotes action. The more I study the Bible and read of the many acts and commandants by God, and the follow the life of Jesus Christ, I become clearer on the repetition of the Bible to explain love in various ways and terms persistently throughout the Bible.

I am no Bible expert, but in my limited study and understanding, I finally am getting a glimpse of what is meant the loosely and frequently used phrase, "God is love." Amazing, I say.

A New Beginning

"Behold, I will do a new thing; now it shall spring forth; shall ye not know it? I will even make a way in the wilderness, and rivers in the desert." **Isaiah 43:19 (KJV)**

God is beginning a new thing. When something is healed, it is like new, like a sore where the infection has stopped and the itching persists, until a crust is formed and falls off. The skin is new underneath and smooth, and must now take on a new color and process. It has gone through a process.

Sometimes, it involves blending in or sometimes it leaves a distinctive scar which serves as a reminder of where you have been and what you have overcome. At best, it reminds us of our Healer, at the very least the One who heals the heart and the body.

The description provided above of the healing process may have been facilitated by a loving caregiver (like a mother, sister, or brother), but this healing soon takes a life on its own, and it's turned into something new. The pain has given breath to new life, to a bloom of new beginning and forwardness of life. It is then when we stop looking around for something that is no longer there.

Coming through healing is complex and simplistic at the same time. In that time of "coming through," we are going through process that seems like it's in slow motion. We only need to call on God, Jesus, Jesus help me! You might wonder when will that that breakthrough happen? When will all that **happen to me, stop hurting me? When will I see the light?**

This is what we expect in the world of instant gratification, but God knows what we need and His timing is not according to our own expectancy. Things began to happen during this process. You become happy about the possibilities, then sad because it seems as if you are stuck. Then there comes the loneliness, the isolation.

And we ask God, why this? But this is all a plan to mold for what God has created you to do. Just continue to walk through.

For example, I remember my time of blessings, when I moved into a new place after my after my last divorce, my daughter was college, and here I was alone. I could hear only the sounds of the house and outside animals and the rain drops.

I said, "Thank You, Lord, for this peace."

Those feelings of loneliness, translated in times of stillness and conversations with God, and I begin to appreciate the blessing that was given. This was time to create and become closer to God in my isolation.

In my physical isolation from others, I became more connected to my creator, and began to experience the incomprehensible love that that I was given, that we all give. But unfortunately at times becomes oblivious to it because of all the distractions in the world. For distractions are useful in keeping us from our destiny, our purpose, our connection with other, and most of all, the connection with our God and Creator.

When I was sitting down to write this book, there were many internal distractions that delayed the process.

I began asking myself, "Who wants to hear your story? Your story is no different from many people. Why are you going to expose your personal business to the world?"

I thought, "My family is going to hate me."

These were some the endless internal negative thoughts that delayed this process and almost made me abort the assignment that God had given me. No one said it would be easy. God did not promise me it would be easy, but it was not easy for many who choose to believe and obey what has they have been assigned to do on this earth walk.

And so, I became isolated for number of reasons. Some by my own doing, and some by circumstance. However, in self-inflicted isolation, I was in the process of changing some relationships, by creating distance and time to promote healing.

If an individual in an environment that feeds and perpetuates the pain, can that be a place of healing? Can healing take place when your mind remembers the trauma or crisis? Healing has to do with renewing of the mind so that you can embrace all yourself.

Healing is what you consciously choose to walk through, because to remain unconscious would be to remain in that pain.

Unconsciousness can be brought to awareness by stating exactly what happened to you or someone else and stating your authentic feelings and emotions about that experience. Until the authenticity of what experienced is fully acknowledged and stated, true healing cannot began.

So, can healing began in the lies? Lies prevent healing. My answer to that is no, because it is the perpetuation of falsehood, and denial of birthright to prosperity and reaching your highest purpose.

Your destiny is stolen because of the refusal to acknowledge the truth and be present in the emotions associated with the truth of that trauma or crisis. Therefore, when no one else is willing to accept that truth, you must be willing, even if it means going into place of isolation. Just remember that you are never alone in that place.

In my isolation, those times when no one calls, no one shows up, and all is quiet are valuable because I am revealed through

God's love and grace. I began to see myself, for who I really am, all my hurt, my pain, but most of all, the beauty. I see how my heart is being molded, how to learn how to love, and have grace even those who have hurt and abused me.

God loves them too and only wants their highest good as well.

This is where my healing began, in the presence if God.

Something that is No Longer There

One day, I was asking my daughter where my nail polish was. I asked her if she borrowed it and she said, "I don't have any polish."

Before, in my former life, living in our other house in my 2nd brief marriage, where I once had 2 daughters, and now I have one to take my nail polish.

My memories all take on a life of their own when the healing is there and the trauma no longer takes over. There was time when I would cringe at the thought of my former life, whether any thought about it, in "good and bad experiences" cause a deep sense of hurt in my heart. But now I find myself looking around for something that is no longer there. It is at that point when I realize that former things were not my own, are not my own, for I am not of myself, but of God, and to God I belong. For the things in this life are temporary—hurt, pain, sorrow. Our time is limited, is a gift from God. We owe all praises to God for His grace and mercy.

In that one second, I understood that this life is not about me. I began to pay attention. I can hear God's voice. I will hear the Spirit guiding me, and I follow courageously, though I do not see. God is in me, in us, in you! Therefore, I must prepare to look forward and no longer look to former things, no more looking around for something that is no longer there or I could miss what is in front of me.

When God Sends a Blessing

When God sends you the blessing you've been waiting for, what are you going to do? Are you going to accept and embrace it or will you reject it?

When thinking about this, I thought about a gift that God was blessing me with, and I was not sure of what it was because it did not look like what I expected, but it was exactly what I needed. And I said these words to myself, **"I don't need to reject the gift, but I don't need to contaminate it either!"**

How was I going to embrace something that I had never experienced, but yet needed and prayed for so long? And there was a voice in my spirit that just told me to, "Walk through it."

In other words, the voice was telling me to walk by faith and not by sight, to trust in the Lord, for He knows what's best for me, and I am covered.

His voice said, "So trust Me, dear child, I love you."

And with that, I gained such peace and understanding, not wondering. What would happen next? It gave me peace and understanding. I did not need to know what would happen next, I only needed to surrender.

But I must walk patiently through it, through the doors and allow things to unfold in their season according to God's will, and not my own. I must to do things in order, not of my own strength, for I am unable, but of the strength by the Holy Spirit which dwells in me and keeps me within the will of God.

Discomfort

Sometimes you have to move to a place of discomfort in order to allow God to give what you want! This is a concept I also heard in a sermon by Sarah Jakes Roberts in 2018. When I heard that, I thought it was really telling me that, "You have to move to place of discomfort in order for God to bless you with what you need!" Because what you want not always not best thing for you.

What is discomfort and what does it feel like? If you stay comfortable, you will never grow. How do you grow when the shoe always fits perfectly, when everything always go your way, and when there are no challenges? Then life is stagnant. It is simply at a standstill, there is no movement because there is no friction, there is no pounding. There is no pressure.

Pressure, friction, and pounding allows us to grow if we work with it. We can become creative and learn to persevere through those challenges.

It has been a challenge for me to grow in different ways. I had grown complacent to getting my way and not having work as hard. I felt that I had arrived after overcoming so many other obstacles in my career and role as a single mother raising my daughter. It had become a challenge for me to communicate with the opposite sex. I found it a difficult subject to pursue the idea of having a community center focused on women and girls dealing with abuse and other difficulties. But I had to move past my comfort zone, to allow a new thing to take root in my life. It was then that I began to gain knowledge of myself. While getting to know myself, I began to see the value in my life experiences.

The Importance of Knowing Your Value

The importance of knowing your value is a critical aspect of your life. Not knowing your value allows you to settle for things that are not for you, taking ownership of things that do not belong to you, and things you never should have been involved in.

I was talking to a friend one day, and we were talking about relationships, and why we are always choosing a certain type of male is less honorable than our being.

We were speaking, about her pending divorce. Her, soon to be, ex-husband had begged her to marry him. In the beginning, she refused married to him, even after pregnancy, but still married. We questioned how the situation got this point of the marriage and then divorce. I concluded, it's about knowing your value. You see, I told her this, "You did not know what you had, but he knew what you had. If you had known what you had, you would not have had him!"

Let me say this one more time, **"You did not know what you had, but he knew what you had. If you had known what you had, you would not have had him!"**

So a lot of times, we settle for less, because we think that's all there is. When God only wants the best for you, His best is beyond what you can imagine or think.

And I say, "Yes, God, I want to be blessed!"

Since you know better, there is no need for shame in mistakes. Count it as learning.

More on Shame - Here Again

What shame causes the pain to perpetuate and infect relationships? This creates a shield or barrier which "guards" the survivor against establishing any relationships of depth. This occurs because to go deep would mean to be vulnerable, transparent, and authentic. And this vulnerability is a threat to causing more pain and the cycles continues. This is the danger of shame.

The person is always worried about being found out. They ask the question, "What will they think of me? Will they think that I am broken and not worth of their love or time? WILL I BE REJECTED?"

While writing this book, someone asked me if they would be in the book. And this person went on to say, on to state, "You have to get someone's permission to write about them." This made me think of how powerful the issue of shame and being "found out" could impact the progression of healing.

Shames prevents many healthy relationships from forming, but instead deception, cover-up, avoidance of issues, and shallow conversations dominate the course of the relationship. To be transparent would mean being vulnerable which could lead to more pain.

This prompted me in my spirit. I said, "God, I need to complete the assignment which you have given me."

It's too many things that need to be said, to help others. It was never about me. I know this, since I have been resistant in being transparent about my own life experiences. It is usually easier to tell a story about someone else rather than focus on yourself. This was a way for me overcome my shame, through transparency. It allows me to be authentic with myself and others. Being authentic with my own feelings allows a place for healing for myself as well as others.

I did not plan to talk so much about shame, but it seems that it is an ongoing theme to many people's pain. In my line of work, as a psychologist, I come in contact with people often suffering from a great deal of emotional pain. And in the process of the discussion, shame is the culprit, which stops the healing. It has been the one factor that has been consistent in most cases of depression, whereas the culprit for anxiety has been fear.

But for now, we will focus on the how shame blocks the path to emotional and psychological healing. Many of the excuses I hear are like, "I'm afraid of what others would think of me if I get help. They will think I am weak, less than a man, that I am weak, or being a crybaby." Or, "What would my husband think of me?" Or, "What would my wife think of me?"

Unfortunately, the truth of the matter is, family and friends probably already notice that something is wrong, because relationships have begun to transform into distant, unhealthy, or non-existent relationships. Individuals begin to isolate, withdraw, and lash out which can lead to more depression and more anxiety. In essence, the pain is being fed poison and becoming more infected.

Here's an analogy that I often tell my patients: "Your emotional pain like anxiety or depression is like an open sore. When you don't treat it and ignore it, the sore becomes more infected, leading to a bigger wound. **The wound only begins to heal when you open the bandage, put on medicine on it, let it get some air, and tend to it daily**—this is the prescription. Now your problem has compounded, because now the emotional pain has caused you to lose relationships, opportunities, and time with family/friends. The infection affects your children, and then their children, until the cycle stops. Healing is process that involves several components. Let us examine some phases of healing:

The Phases of Healing (The AOCA Theory - L. Young, 2017)

1) **ACKNOWLEDGMENT** of Problem – Acknowledging that there is pain, that there is a wound
2) **ORIGIN** of pain – Where is the pain coming from; what started the pain, opened the wound
3) **CHOICE** – Make a choice, a decision to overcome the pain and heal the internal wound
4) **ACTION** – Make movement toward healing, take one step at time, began your healing (what is your Action Plan?)

ACKNOWLEGDEMENT of the problem: Can you heal if you do not know that there is a problem? The answer is absolutely not! What if you are oblivious to the problem, and don't understand why you are going into this continuous loop of things in life, where everything keeps changing around you, but the outcomes in your life remain the same? Nothing is changing, Are you missing the point, are you missing what's wrong, are you only scratching the surface of pain? Your pain goes deeper than your conscience would allow you to go, but the subconscious mind orchestrates behaviors that lead to the same behavioral outcome over and over again. How do you get to the deep layer of that pain that your conscience won't allow you to face, to discover? One clue would be to look at your pattern of behaviors that you are enacting in your relationships with others. What is it that you desire? What is it that you fear? What is it that you are running from? What is the worst thing that can happen if you stop running? Can you stop trying to be the leader for one second and listen to what is God telling you, but yet you have not seen nor listened? Be still, rest and hear what has been spoken in your spirit.

Perhaps this is the one of the benefits of meditation. It provides us with clarity to distinguish our voice from God's voice, his desires from our own, and His guidance from our own direction. Clarity is where we acknowledge the pain, because you become knowledgeable of the pain and begin to seek the path of its origin.

And with this, true healing can begin. In the previous chapters, I talked about what got me to this this point to write this book on healing, how some of those losses and crises were just a blessing in disguise. At the end of the day, they worked out for my good.

What happened is that it gave me a way to begin my path in listening to God and watching how He was moving in my life despite the circumstances I was placed in. It allowed me to see only the tip of the iceberg of His love for me, and for all. With this acknowledgment of pain from persistent loss, death of family/friends and relationships, divorce, and death within my body (miscarriages). All of this could only to death of my will in the natural, leading to depression. While in session with a client, she was balling her eyes out, explaining that she had asked for a healing, but was still not healed. She was saying that she asked the pastor for healing, saying, "but I was not healed."

So I asked her how much of her emotional pain had been revealed or acknowledged. Was she still covering something up while asking for healing? And she sat there silently, so I proceeded and asked her, "How then will you or anyone else know what to heal if you don't reveal it?"

So I gave her this scenario: "What if you have a sore on your hand and a small cut, but you only show the small cut to the doctor and conceal the large infected sore with clothing. The doctor gives you medicine for the scratch, and you think you are now healed.

But you are not because you concealed the infected area that could not be healed because it was not shown to the doctor."

Emotional pain, though not seen directly, can fester into something bigger if you do not stop it and reveal it, so that we can heal it. That's why honest acknowledgment of pain is an integral part of this process of becoming whole (healing).

ORIGIN of the pain: Where did your pain start? Did it start with the life-changing event, or did it start with something prior to that time? What happened? What is the origin of the pain? The origin is the beginning of it all. It began in your mind with how you process the information, the event—whether it was shock, betrayal, disappointment, rejection, horror, fear, or physical pain. Even that can be conceptualized as ongoing, because when the stimuli or the thing causing the pain is gone, the memory is engraved in the core of our psychological being.

The issue here is how do we reverse that? How do we respond to that? We go back to identify the very core of where it all began. Finding and locating the origin of the wound is an integral part of beginning the healing process.

CHOICE is at the very core of all. It involves making a decision after you have acknowledged the pain and located the origin of the pain. What are you going to do about it? How does your story end?

In essence, how do you defeat the enemy of pain? How do you overcome it? Jesus had already overcome the world and he knows your pain. Are you going to bear it all yourself or reach for help before you drown and self-destruct in a sea of depression? This is your time, this is your path, and your opportunity to regain power, to take back your power, and renew your strength by renewing your mind. Use your pain as a means to develop parts of your inner self and strength that you did not know existed. Your crisis has created something new through pressure, through death. You have a choice to **stand still** or **take action**. Whatever it is you always make a choice, whether you do nothing or choose door number 1, number 2, or number 3, the power is within you to acknowledge your power of choice.

ACTION to put in motion your journey to healing. Placing one tiny step in front of the other is the beginning of action steps you take in your life. Your choices determine which action you take, which path you will follow, and how you will proceed on your journey. How does it benefit you to do nothing? What is your action plan? What steps will you take to begin with in the first place? How do you ask for help? Who can you trust? Help is always there, but you have be still and listen so that you may take the proper action.

Perseverance

With healing I knew that I had to persevere in living in reaching for my goals and making new goals because what I once perceived as a failure is no longer perceived as a failure. But now I see it as a learning experience and an opportunity to share with others how I overcame depression, anxiety, doubt, and fear to begin a new life, to have the courage to love again, to dream again, to laugh again, and to give again.

This is how God sees us. We are loved despite our mistakes and perceived failures. We are whole to God and He waits for us to call on him for help. God graciously helps us and blesses us when we do not deserve it. It is by God's grace that we succeed, and it's by God's love that we live and thrive! This is motivation for me to exercise perseverance when things do not seem to be going as I envision. The determination to keep going is predicated on the belief in God's promise for my life.

In the beginning of this book, I discussed a lot about my relationships, the losses, and pain associated therein. However, out of those ashes there was beauty for the outcome. My resilience in my trauma allowed me to persevere toward my destiny, and my belief in God's promise propelled it all.

Perseverance and resilience are not the same, but they are essential elements to your healing. What is perseverance? It is the determination or the steady persistence in a course of action especially in the time of difficulty, discouragement, or obstacles.

Resilience

Resilience involves the capacity to quickly recover from difficulties. It's toughness. It is my belief that perseverance can build or help develop some form of resilience.

Whether you are discussing the resiliency of the mind or the body, a toughness is developed overtime from experiences because it is predicated on the belief that "things will get better" or that, "I will get through this somehow."

There is a mental toughness that develops as well a physical toughness that develops. You see this in overcomers, in athletes, scientists, and in artists, just to name a few.

In my own life experiences, despite the negative events which cause fear, trauma, distrust, and doubt, I usually held the belief that somehow, some way things would get better.

At other times, I lost hope and fell into a deep depression and stopped talking to God as often. Yes, I admit it. I was angry at God and did not forgive myself for a long time. I blamed everyone else and myself too. I punished myself for far longer than I had too when God had already forgiven me when I first asked him.

What are you punishing yourself for? Why haven't you forgiven yourself?

What do you do next? Do you share your experiences to help others heal or do keep it to yourself? Often, we keep our experiences ourselves, but why? To share is not always on a large scale, but many times our subtleties is how others watch us go through our experiences. As they watch, they sometimes learn vicariously. They watch as we maneuver through the paths of crises and trauma by way of perseverance and resilience. Our healing not only affects us, but it also affects others, which is affecting the world.

As individuals perpetuate in sickness without healing, so does the perpetual sickness persist in the forms of fear, which leads to anxiety, anger, sadness, depression, rejection, resentment, discontentment, inferiority, and feelings of superiority. If you investigate all the above negative feelings, thoughts, and emotions, you find that they stem from pain of an open wound that has not healed. Are you experiencing any of those feelings? Where did they come from?

Helping others promotes healing. This is psychological understanding that a coping strategy for persons who are depressed would be to focus externally and less internally. For example, to examine how you could help others in a crisis who are in need of some form of help. This is how we walk through the healing, this is how we come through healing: we focus on something on the outside of ourselves. We focus on God and his way for us. We mediate, be still and listen. We do this, because we have tried doing it our way and it did not work. God was just waiting on us to pray and call out His name and depend on him wholly, listening what He whispers to us in our spirit.

Understand that your times of loneliness are just opportunities to listen and speak with Him, and listen to what your life is purposed for. And as we began to this, as you began to do this, and as I did this; I began to experience a portion of God's greatness and love for my life and what he has for me. It became real and I did not feel so alone anymore, for that feeling was just an illusion because God was there all alone, always there to listen, always there to comfort, as an ever-present help!

'Coming through' is a means of action that allows surrendering our will to God's will for our lives. Even in the psychological principles, when reaching beyond self and channeling energies, away from "persistent self-consciousness" this lifts the depression, lifts the anxiety. Well, you may ask why I speak these concepts—anxiety and depression. These concepts cause the infection to persist in an emotional wound and prevents healing.

Let's explore depression first. What is it? I will give you my definition: depression is anger and disappointment turned inward or directed at the self. It could come in part from un-forgiveness of self and associated emotions like guilt or shame.

Thus, depression symptoms include: feelings of hopelessness, helplessness, negative thoughts, restlessness, excessive worry, difficulty in making decisions, feeling unsure of yourself, loss of interest, isolation, thought of death, worthlessness, and excessive sleep or lack of sleep (APA, 2013).

You see how this is an element that prevents healing? Now let's look at anxiety. Anxiety comes from the emotion of fear coupled with expectancy.

Let me repeat that again, "Fear coupled with expectancy" leads to anxiety, or breeds anxiety. Let's explore some symptoms of anxiety. They include similar symptoms to depression. Someone with anxiety may experience restlessness, excessive rumination, irritability, anger with others, jumpiness, isolation, loss of interest, obsessive-compulsive behaviors, racing thoughts, and fatigue. These are two things, anxiety and depression, that prevents us from healing. This could go on for years and years until death.

That's why it is important to acknowledge your pain, instead of saying, "I'm okay" when genuinely you are not okay. Part of coming through the pain involves acknowledging and identifying the pain. Work through the steps of the **ACOA** theory, as discussed above. In healing, there is a process by which we encounter different phases.

To me, it seems like having the flu. When you think you are feeling better you get up and start coming out of your shell, you start creating, start loving again. And then boom!- you get knocked down again because you thought you were fully healed, but as you start to encounter circumstances, relationship, it challenges the parts of you that you did not know were scarred.

I remember when I had the flu. After a couple of days of rest, I felt better and starting overexerting myself, then suddenly, I could not get out of bed the next morning. I was super tired and stayed in the bed for few days except to get something to eat, go to the bathroom, or shower.

I was forced to be still because I had to acknowledge my vulnerability and my need for others to help me.

Now you feel your judgment has failed you and now you don't even trust yourself to tell you how you are feeling!

In reality there is an Intermediate Phase to that healing where you began to feel better, then you began to venture out into world again by mean of exploration, creativity, and interpersonal relationships. However, during that intermediate phase you are knocked back into a state of illness, feeling as if you were never well, and knocked in state of awareness to re-evaluate (Re-evaluation phase).

It is here that you began to examine what you missed and why you missed it, therefore entering into: Resting Phase. This is the time that your rest in action, thoughts, and carefully listen to who you are. This is like when you have the flu. You rest after that first bout of feeling well and with sudden sickness, you rest.

Then there is the Healing Phase, where you are actually healing, feeling like yourself, appreciative of life and opportunities ahead. You are optimistic and looking forward to the future. With God, he has a way for us to heal, but we don't always see his work and his power as we are challenged along our journey of life. Sometimes our most challenging moment brings out the best in us, allows us to be still and rest, to mediate on what our purpose is in this life. Otherwise, we are either moving too fast, moving too slow, or stagnant without purpose. We might be existing and not living with purpose until a crisis or tragedy takes us by surprise and causes us to move into a different space, even if that means we become broken in order to become whole again.

What has happened in your trauma, tragedy, or crisis that moved you toward your destiny? Would you change anything about that circumstance that moved you? Do you think you would be pursuing your destiny/dream had you not experience that? What phase of healing are you at?

REACHING PROSPERITY

"For I know the thoughts that I think toward you, says the Lord, thoughts of peace, and not of evil, to give you a future and a hope."
Jeremiah 29:11 (NKJV)

What is prosperity? Many times, when we experience a crisis that causes pain—whether prolonged, acute, or otherwise—we are often discouraged about our future. We have the feeling that the crisis has ended our life, but, it hasn't. This is an opportunity to birth something new out of your pain, something beautiful, if you embrace it.

Well, you may ask, how exactly do I do that? How do I begin to live again, feel again? Because right now, I'm numb. How do I love again, and most of all, how do I create something from my brokenness? Do I ignore the pain and keep going like superwoman until I crack? Of course, you know the answer to those questions is an absolute, "NO!"

What is it that I must do to live a prosperous, fulfilling life? This brings us back to what is prosperity? According to the dictionary or online Google express, prosperity is a successful, flourishing or thriving condition, especially in financial respects; good fortune.

This definition is a general one, but limiting. Let me explain. Prosperity is synonymous with the concept of success. Well, we all have different definitions of success and how we identity success. For some, success is obtaining a lot of money, but what is a lot of money for one person, is little for another. Success may involve being a good parent, a great spouse, or a great entrepreneur.

The point I am making here is you must define for yourself beyond your imagination what prosperity is to you. Then you aim for it, work towards it, speak it, breathe it, and live until it becomes a part of your being. This is how you start with you healing.

But what I am going to explain is that your mind controls your behavior and determines the action which you will take.

For taking no action is still an action. It is still a choice. If you believe that your life is over and speak it, you are creating your reality for yourself, for your future, and possibly for your offspring.

You are no island but you are connected to others, and your action or non-action impacts others as well. So when I speak of embracing prosperity through wholeness, it means that we should embrace what God has given us: another day, another breath, life in your body. Therefore, you are not over, you are not broken, you are whole and don't even know it because you survived it (the pain, crisis, or trauma).

That was then, and this is now. You are out of that situation or circumstance. Because you are whole, you must embrace the gifts that lay in your continual healing. You are still here for a reason, and now it's up to you to find your purpose, so you ask, "What has God purposed for my life?" What was I supposed to learn from that experience? How can I help others through their pain? How can I embrace my situation and grow from it?

So in your beginning into this new life, after the crisis, after the trauma, at what point do you acknowledge that you need others to assist you in your journey and to learn humility in order to reach out for others for help? Asking for help is a humble act to do, but it's also a smart move and growth move. This is when you are beginning to understand that you are not alone and others can learn from your story, others can learn from your journey if you are willing to share, and be transparent.

That was the most difficult part about writing this. I was trying to figure out how much of my story you needed to know in order to be helpful without getting bogged down with too many unnecessary details. Sometimes the details are less important than the story as a whole and how it affected you and how you got through it all. As you know, I talked a lot about divorce and equated it with failure many times, but it is not a failure; it does not make me a failure.

I now see it as an opportunity to really know who I am and get to where I am going, what to avoid and how to avoid distractions that would abort my destiny. The thing about divorce, is that many times we pick our spouse without confirming it with God, so we don't always make the best choice. Though I was hurt mentally, emotionally, and physically, it was not necessary that I stay there. I was still alive. So I was not broken. I only felt like I was.

God had delivered me from an unhealthy, abusive relationship. He was always there to help me. This help came at the time when I did not know I needed help and when I did not know how to pray for the help that I needed.

Our healing is there waiting for us on the other side of the pain. It is like a mirrored reflection and the illusion of being broken on the physical side and wholeness present on the mirrored side. What we see and feel is not always what we get.

This brokenness is only a temporary feeling that we have in life. It is meant to be temporary, but we feed our brokenness because this is what society has taught us to do.

Now, I am not saying that we should ignore our pain, but I am saying begin to embrace each day that you wake, knowing that you have another opportunity to live, change, and to create positive action in your life and in the world.

So what next? This is time to meditate and to look at what you dreamed of before you were hurt. Though you have been transformed by you experiences, your experiences do not predict your future and do not determine your destiny.

Some say that your destiny has already been determined and that God's grace is what will allow your dreams to come to pass by your belief. Your belief creates your reality, remember, I AM that I AM. My father used always say this to me, and I would look at him strangely because I did not understand what he was speaking of. I knew that this was a something that was stated from the Bible.

I am a visual person, and sometimes learn better when I see something put plainly so that I can understand it. So this is what I what I am saying, see below:

THOUGHTS → BELIEF → ACTION

This is based on concepts taken from Cognitive Behavioral Theory (CBT). Cognitive Behavior Theory is a psychological theory that explains how thinking affect behaviors and how the behaviors can be modified if we change the way we think.

There are several different cognitive behavioral theories, but here I will explain the basic constructs. It refers to cognitions thinking which consist of a person's thoughts, beliefs, how they process information.

So if you believe that your life will never get better, likely your behaviors will manifest as such, and your life probably won't get better. Your belief promotes certain cognitions which create some type of action. The outcome is one of your choosing whether you realize it or not. Therefore, the healing the mind and spirit is a critical part of formulating our thoughts, because our thoughts can promote destiny or kill destiny.

The choice is yours; what are you going to do? Are you going to embrace the promise of prosperity? Will you reach beyond your belief and embrace all that is good and pure and create something, a new beginning for your life?

This is what I did. This is I chose to do. Whatever was given to me by God in the beginning of my life, I felt it coming back: my passion for people, my passion to help children and help women. Helping women was an added to component what was placed on my life in form of destiny.

I initially feared sharing some experiences, because I was afraid of how I would be perceived. There was shame and guilt, but no more. It is more like an unexpected gift that I have been blessed to share. To speak with an audience frankly about abuse without feeling as if I had to hide my face due to being ashamed or guilty of what had happened to me is freeing.

On the surface, things may seem like they are changing or progressing, but take a step and eventually you will find yourself in another place, at another level, and be there before you know it by the grace of God. Continue to persevere and believe in what is real to you, believe in your dream, because it was put there for a reason. It was placed there for you to fulfil. Be resilient despite the obstacles that are before you.

In conclusion: ***Healing is a process. Be patient. Rest, meditate, pray, and listen to the Spirit of God.***

Protection, Mercy, and Grace- God's Healing Gifts

Many times, we become overwhelmed with the work, the loneliness, the isolation of the process associated with healing. We began to feel like we want to give up, because we feel so all alone, forgetting that we have come out of such a crisis by only grace and mercy.

And then we begin to do the work. It feels so overwhelming, but we had forgotten about it or had not yet discovered it!

Maybe we got caught up in the busyness of our everyday life or chasing the dreams and desires of others, not your own. There are many distractions as we go through this life, trying to understand our purpose, what the creator desires for us to complete while we are here. The problem is that some of us never get to that point because we focused on the wrong thing, the wrong line of questioning.

We are focused on the problem, the physical problem itself. We are not focused on the deeper element that got us to that problem, the spiritual aspect, such as what are we supposed to be learning as result of "that problem" or what is the universe trying to tell us about ourselves.

Reflections

How is this experience shaping you? Are you paying attention? Why does it seem that same problems continue to occur time and time again? What is it that I'm missing? What is the lesson in this crisis or problem? I did not cause it to occur – or did I? Have you gone through this or something similar before? What did you learn? Do you consider yourself stronger, more resilient, and more of a believer of miracles?

_____

_____

_____

_____

_____

This is the time to pay attention to the purpose and the lesson. When you pay attention to what life is telling you about yourself, you begin to take on a whole new perspective, one of understanding and humility. Your vision becomes broader and your grace become more extended, as you learn that judgment is yours to give when lack understanding of a complete situation.

Many times as women, we feel that we need someone to make us complete as women, however, being a wife and mother does not completely define you. We are made complete in and by God.

This is how I felt for many years, but now I know better, that I limited the definition of myself. I had to come to understand that I am wonderfully made by my Creator.

For David wrote in Psalms 139:14, "I praise you because I am fearfully and wonderfully made; your works are wonderful, I know that full well." For in the beginning, we were created and belong to Creator (Isaiah 55:4).

There are many phases that we experience in this life, but one confidence for sure is that God promises to never change. For in all things, God is faithful. In short, you are never alone. In your healing, prosperity is around the corner waiting for you. For in your healing, you discover something new about yourself and about your existence in the world. You learn that you are never in any situation alone. Your aloneness is simply an illusion, a lie and trick that deceives you into believing in limitation. I had to learn this. When I discovered my power and how my voice could propel it, I began to reach out for help.

In reaching out for help, I learned the strength of my heart in accepting help. For with the courage in doing something even when afraid, my life began to change and take new form.

I continue to walk and live, and it's with humility that I share my stories. I discovered when we share we are building bridges to help others out of their crises and sorrow. This is what prompted me to write this book, and to begin a foundation (The Sérah Foundation, Inc.) dedicated to the woman and girls who are survivors of domestic abuse and other abuses.

This was a leap of faith and to sit here and write this book, trying to figure out why so many projects have been delayed in my vision for this organization. I know it's only been a year, but somehow, I feel that more should have been done to help the shelters in way of donations, fundraisers, and so forth.

But I know it is coming. I simply had to begin to walk and God would complete the rest. It is at forefront of my mind. I meet with women frequently who have been a victims of childhood sexual abuse, domestic violence, or a sexual assault of some nature. It seems as if God is reminding me every week that I need to continue in that work. That is why I am so adamant about wanting to stop talking and to actually get the work done. I need to begin this work, because perhaps it will never be complete.

In thinking about the things we want to do in this life, we have to clarify what we want. What is our purpose and what is our expected outcome? The outcome can occur in a number of ways depending on the approach that we take. But we must take the first step and begin the work in order for anything to happen. For without movement, there is no action. And all movement creates progress.

That's why movement has to be **strategic, consistent, and definite**. How do you complete all 3 at one time? Can you do all 3 at one time? It that possible or even necessary? What is strategy? **Strategy** is a plan or an approach to a problem or project. **Consistency** is the practice of doing something over and over again in a specific way, time, or situation. To be **definite** means clarity and being clear-cut in what is you are seeking, trying to achieve, or what your expectancy is.

However, it seems when you get closer to your goal, it seems harder, and the more distractions come pouring in.

This is why we must hold on and do whatever it takes to reach your goal using the gift that God has given you to share with the world.

This was my experience while writing this book. Many distractions came into play as I was getting to a point of reaching my goal and bringing everything together, it seemed as in that 10th hour I began to feel discouraged, filled with negative thoughts. There were so many thoughts that would have me stop this work and abort what God has given me to share with you.

You might start to have thoughts like, "Why am I doing this? No one wants to hear what I have to say, or there are a thousand books that talks about healing." Remember these are all lies and distractions to discourage you from your work.

For it is written, if you become weary in well-doing, you will be rewarded (Galatians 6:9, KJV).

In this life, there is good and all bad. Some trials are there create a greater you.

Right now in this moment, in this very day, you are what you tell yourself. You are what God has told you, and nothing less. Therefore, we must be steadfast in obedience so that we can hear our Lord and hear the direction that God is providing for us.

For greater is He that is in us, than is he who is in the world (**1 John 4:4, KJV**).

God is in us, we are his children, but we walk away at times and ignore His word, his voice, his commandment, and his instruction. It is by God's love and grace that helps us before we ask for it, before we know we need it, or before know to call out his name. "Help, help me, Lord!"

So in understanding the nature of why we must be **Definite** about intention, **Consistent** in our belief, and **Strategic** in our actions, this the way we create an authentic movement toward healing God's way that creates prosperity.

One of the quickest ways to procrastination is being unsure, being inconsistent, and having no plan or strategy in getting there. Going back and forth, being "wishy-washy" or double-minded is not productive or healthy at times.

Your healing is based on a belief that you have about yourself or situation in your mind. Therefore, it is important that good information replaces the negative and distorted thoughts we have given ourselves or that others have to us, so there is a renewing of the mind.

My belief, while going through an abusive relationship was challenged by myself, and by others. Though well-meaning, people would ask, "Are you overacting? Are you moving too fast? Or that's probably not the way you think it is."

You see, what you know about yourself prior to abuse (your spirit knows it even if you are not conscious of it) is that you are strong, beautiful, capable. Maybe you did not know these things because no one ever told them to you, but you know how you felt when something bad or derogatory was said to you. Perhaps, *it did not sit well with you*. Some go in sorrowful depression, or sickness.

The reason is that your Spirit could not take the lies that were being thrown at you about yourself. It was screaming and fighting against that, that's why it did not sit well with you, because you knew that it was not something right about that situation.

"What you are carrying on your shoulders is what you are attracting." This statement came to me when talking to a friend about my past relationships. I was discussing what I was attracting, why was attracting, or attracted to those men who were not supportive. Why was I the giver in the situation, even when they started out giving? And I came to this conclusion. They knew something about me that I did not know about myself. What is that they knew about me that I did not know? They knew my value, my worth, and knew that they gotten me for a cheaper price, all because I was ignorant of who I was, whose I was, and the greatness that was an integral part of my being. I did not know, but they knew.

Well, you may ask, what is the problem with not knowing? Well, the danger with not knowing who you are leads to settling for situations which you would have never settled, if you had who you were.

Charity's Story

Charity explains, "There was a conscious act to make me feel belittled, in the behaviors that he portrayed, the infidelity, the abuse, the criticisms, almost succeeded. These acts almost made me stay in that abusive situation, because I felt unworthy and ashamed. This man, my ex-husband, was desperate to have control of something, and that something was me. His anxiety had gotten the best of him, lost control and became impulsive in his actions. He had no hope because he have placed his hope and trust in himself. He trusted only what he could see and feel. I believe this led to his emptiness."

Charity further explains, "I am not just talking about myself and my personal situation, I am talking about how anxiety fills an individual when he or she is lost and is on empty, trying to fill that emptiness with alcohol, drugs, sex, and food."

What seems great and perfect to them, they began to covet and therefore tries to degrade or invade its existence, to make themselves feel better or whole.

The anxiety comes when they feel they are losing. The woman is beaten when she decides to leave as less attention given to the abuser because of circumstances (i.e., pregnancy, miscarriages, family). She was in a cage created by her husband and her mind.

Charity explains, "I believe this is what he did to control his world, because he had no control over himself. I remember seeing the emptiness as I looked into his glaring eyes, they were, dark, empty and distant as attacked me, asking me in that moment was I going to leave him." He was lost. Yes, he was lost!

Healing can only come by acknowledging that there is problem. The problems with lost people is they attract other lost people. What I have just described to you in the above is a story of 2 people, the abuser and the survivor.

Charity was lost, because she did not know her greatness, but others did. Because of her ignorance she placed herself unknowingly in situations that could derail her life or possibly kill her.

The other person described was a man (abuser) who was lost. He found what he thought he needed and held onto it, in the form of woman. But what he needed was healing for his soul, what he needed was God. The woman could not make him whole, no human can make you whole, you are completed only through the blood of Jesus, the grace of God.

Silence in a New Beginning

Silence is defined as the still place in our minds, the still place in the physical environment, it is a resting state of being; it is quietness on multiple levels. This is how I define silence. According to Merriam Webster Dictionary, Silence is defined as:

1. Forbearance from speech or noise:
2. MUTENESS Absence of sound or noise:
3. STILLNESS Absence of mention: SECRECY; OBSCURITY; OBLIVION

Is silence a bad thing? It could be if you don't appreciate it. Some gifts may be gaining more information, more insight, and guidance from the right source: God. Hearing what God is telling your spirit about the situation, your decisions, and the next move.

Silence in isolation is an opportunity to listen and be still in a way that allows you to get to know yourself. It can be a powerful tool in a world that fills us with multiple distractions, such as television, cell phone, radio, iPad, iPod, Alexa, Google, etc. and the list goes on with the multiple chatrooms, social media, YouTube, Facebook, and so on.

Silence is not looked upon as something being good, but rather, if you are silent, you must be weak, lonely, and boring.

When in reality, it could mean that you are strong, content, and highly creative. Silence allows the creative gifts to come forward, if we are willing to embrace them, then we begin to understand who we are authentically, to really see ourselves *for the very first time*. I begin to see myself. It is then, when I saw myself, that I could begin fully living.

In truly knowing who we are, seeing ourselves, then we can begin to live fully, without fear, and leap into our destiny, to love, to fight, to pursue, to work, and to be still in silence.

Being still in silence is like a battery recharging itself, reviving itself. You are revitalizing your spirit to allow you to fight to win, to win your true self, to be courageous in following through on you assignment that was given to you be the creator.

This is an integral part of your continued healing. Though the new skin has grown over the scar, the deeper wound is still very fragile and would need time to heal those deep parts, especially if the wound had festered for a long period of time.

While on my journey to healing, it was a year of soul-searching, devotion and talking with God, and a lot of psychotherapy. God works through people.

During that year, I learned a lot about myself, what I believe, and how much I am not alone, and how much God really loves me. I still cannot describe the depth of love and grace I began to feel from my Creator. In trying to describe to another person in conversation, I held in tears of joy and overwhelming love of the salvation and deliverance of my life. The deliverance from something that I could not have orchestrated myself, could not have conceptualized it, or planned it...

"I surrender, I surrender my will for Your (God's) will for my life," is my mantra. *(Alex Young).*

Healing, Not Perfection

At the end of day, you don't have to be perfect. Most of us think, "Now that I feel better than myself, and I am healing," feeling unbroken, that everything in our lives has to be perfect.

This could not be more untrue.

Healing is process where you have your initial breakthrough of forgiveness, responsibility, and insight. When a scar is healing, the skin is no longer broken on top (as discussed earlier), but there is still a process that must continue in order to facilitate further healing.

In our emotional, psychological, and spiritual walk to continue living on this earth with hope, we find it sometimes difficult to locate the tools needed for the next steps of healing.

However, God is there to help us, but we must believe that we can be healed. We must believe that what we desire and ask within the will for our lives will come to pass.

We must be believe what we ask, and that mind change (in psychology), cognitive change or cognitive restructuring, we will see change occur beyond what we believed initially.

Have you ever been working toward a goal, but did not believe or have faith that you would reach it? If so, what happened? Did you find yourself giving up way to soon? Becoming discourage too easily?

What would have happened if you continued to believe despite all obstacles, distractions, setbacks, and continued to work and pray and follow your spirit? What you think the outcome would have been?

This is not meant to imply that you have to do all the work, but I am suggesting something that has been proven time and time again in the secular world and spiritual world. What you believe impacts your life, you destiny, your outcome.

What you have in your mind is the most powerful tool and weapon. You have to succeed and become prosperous.

Your healing is dictated by what you believe, and what you believe can either limit you or propel you.

I had a close family member who would always say to me, "God only wants your highest good," and I could not understand that in midst of trauma, my losses, and depression. But my spirit caught a hold to what she was saying.

That one statement was telling me that God loves you, you are going be okay, all is good, and that you are going to become greater than your present circumstance.

That one statement resonated with my spirit when I could not hear it with my flesh. My subconscious mind heard it when my conscious mind was deaf to the meaning and understanding of it all.

You see, I would not have been writing this book if I had not experienced significant change and loss during the years 2014-2016. Those two years of my life (as discussed earlier) were preceptors from my history and previous life experiences.

Was I there to give and teach something to individuals who came in and connected with me, or was I even supposed to be there in the first place?

Even if I was not supposed to be there in the first place, God was working all that for God, for those who were involved in the circumstance. This is difficult for me to understand because my thoughts are that of a human. As long as there is life, there is a time for healing and redemption. It is always there. We are distracted from its presence. We are distracted because of a number of factors in our life, whether it's our upbringing, our experiences, or our lack thereof.

At the end of the day, it is our beliefs (however you call it, thinking, feelings, emotions), that impact the outcome.

Belief is the foundation of our outcomes and the fuel behind our actions. When we have a belief in something that is part of our destiny, then it will occur. If we don't believe that it will happen for us, then it probably will not happen. Many times we pray for things to occur in our lives, but then we don't believe in what we are praying for. Think that it is simply supposed to happen because we prayed when all along we were not believing the words which we were saying. We acted as if we are surprised when things don't happen when ask and do not believe. Our belief is not settled in our hearts and minds. We are saying vain words at times. Yes, what you say is powerful, but what you belief is even more powerful. For what you speak is what is in your belief system.

Healing is a process, but it's not linear—it's rather circular and continuous process. Healing has many layers and complexities that we are somewhat unaware of. I began to learn of the complexities of my healing as I became stronger and gained more knowledge about my pain's origin. It seems the stronger I got, the more difficult the process became. Perhaps, because I viewed it or perceived it as a setback to my wholeness.

I thought that once I was stronger, I would not slip back into those patterns of behavior that were destructive to my being. But this is what I learned: I lacked self-awareness of what those behaviors were until I was faced with the same lesson but in a new strength, and different level of awareness. A level of awareness that would allow me to cry and to feel my pain, to not silence myself and to speak out and speak up about what was really bothering me!

I gained an awareness of my imperfections, and that was okay. I no longer would punish and beat myself up for my mistakes, for loving or dating the wrong person. I just knew this one thing: that I need to just get up and keep on moving. I needed to keep moving and experience the moment, every good thing of it, every bad thing of it, and all the gray areas.

I needed to FEEL what was in the moment. Because I knew that part of my pain was not allowing myself to feel it, to acknowledge it, and therefore process it. How can you process something that you don't even acknowledge is there?

How can you process trauma if you hide from its existence? You avoid its presence and therefore it creates a bigger impact on your life and consumes you. This is what I felt happened to me. I was consumed in a shell of pain and trauma and therefore I recreated this scenario throughout my life and my life choices.

Therefore, I realized that principles discussed in the *ACOA Theory* would be useful in continued healing and rediscovery of self. Yes, there is life after pain; and yes, there is life after trauma. God is the Healer of All!

CONCLUSION

"Beloved, I wish above all things that thou mayest prosper and be in health, even as thy soul prospereth." 3 John 1:2 (KJV)

If you have not figured it out, "Charity's Story" was my story. Through my experiences and growth toward a closer relationship with God, I had to learn forgiveness and compassion. These were the two elements that were essential to my healing.

Though my family traditions and belief systems influenced some of my decisions and directions in my life that sometimes lead to traumatic experiences; all family teachings were not negative. I learned perseverance, hard work, about God, and love–these things stayed with me to my core. These essential elements allowed me to be resilient in times of turmoil. How that was conveyed was not always clear or perfect. The people (my mother, father, and people coming in and out my life in seasons) who influence me are part who I am today, what pushed me toward my destiny that God had for me. Without those experiences, I would not been shaped into who I am—I embrace them all. I learned, I loved, I forgave and therefore I felt compassion!

What I have learned is that everyone has their own story and struggles, including my mother, my biological father, and my stepfather. This is where I learned to have compassion regarding behaviors that I encountered, and to forgive spoken and unspoken words and actions for things which I felt could have been done differently. The bottom line is people cannot give you everything that you need, but what you have gotten from them is enough, because God is your provider and your experiences have prepared you for a God-driven purpose.

I had to learn this on my journey, and with this, I learned love, for God is Love. With Love, this is where your healing begins, and this where Prosperity begins!

REFERENCES

American Psychiatric Association (2013). Post- Traumatic Stress Disorder (PTSD). In *Diagnostic and statistical manual of mental disorders* (5th Ed.).

Author Unknown. *God, a Marine and a Spider Web.*

Beck, A. (1967). *Depression: Causes and treatment.* Philadelphia, PA: University of Pennsylvania Press.

The Bible. King James Version/Amplified Bible Parallel Edition, Large Print (1987). Zondervan. Grand Rapids, Michigan 49530, USA. www.zondervan.com.

The Bible. New King James Version. YouVersion. Life.Church, 2008-2016.

The Bible. AMPC Version. YouVersion. Life.Church, 2008-2016.

The Bible, HCSB Version. YouVersion. Life.Church, 2008-20016.

Egnew, T. R. (2005). *The Meaning of Healing: Transcending Suffering.* Annals of Family Medicine, Vol. 3 (3), May/June.

Frankl, V. (2018). Viktor *Frankl's Logotherapy.* Retrieved from goyourownway.org on 9/2/2018.

Greater Good Magazine: Science- Based Insight for Meaningful Use. *(2018). What is Forgiveness?* Retrieved on September 5, 2018, from https://greatergood.berkeley.edu/topic/forgiveness/definition.

In Cooperation with Editors of Merriam- Webster. (2000). *Webster's New Explorer Large Print Dictionary.* Federal Street Press. Springfield, Massachusetts

Roberts, S. J. (2017, April 20). *The Uncomfortable Advantage* [Video File]. Retrieved from https://www.youtube.com/watch?v=pLdyllcO2s&t1963s

Siegel, B. (2018). *The Art of Healing in Podcast.* Retrieved on July 4, 2018 from https://itunes.apple.com/us/podcast/maryannelive-radio-show/id1169355348?mt2&=100041190022.

Ventegolt, S.; Anderson, N. J.; and Merrick, J. (2003). *Holistic Medicine III: The Holistic Process Theory of Healing.* The Scientific World Journal, 3, 1138-1146.

Wommack, A. *The Good Report: God Wants You Well* [Pamphlet]. Andrew Wommack Ministries, Colorado Springs, CO. www.awmi.net

**This is a not a research paper. I am sure there are many more articles and research about healing, but I wanted this book to be based on my experiences how healing process was me through the inspiration of God's word, The Bible.